MASTERING FINANCIAL ANALYTICS

Prof. Dr. R. Gopal,

Prof. Dr. Vani Kamath,

Dr. Priya Vij

INDIA • SINGAPORE • MALAYSIA

Contents

About the Authors

Prof. Dr. R. Gopal

Prof. Dr. R. GOPAL is an Engineer from I.I.T., Kharagpur in Mechanical Engineering. Subsequently he did his MBA, ICWA, PhD and Post-Doctoral Research degree -- D. Litt. Currently, Prof. Dr. R. Gopal is the Director, Head of the Department & Former Dean D.Y. Patil Deemed to be University, School of Management. (School of Arts and Commerce).

He has more than 27 years of Corporate Experience at Bush India Ltd., Larsen and Toubro, Tata Consultancy Services and at Siemens. Additionally, he has more than 30 years of Teaching Experience in various B Schools in and around Mumbai in the areas of Marketing, Finance, and General Management etc. He was also the visiting faculty in several B Schools in USA. In the USA, he has conducted several programs on topics like "How to Business in India". He has also published more than 200 research papers both in Indian and foreign journals. He has been awarded the BEST OUTSTANDING RESEARCH PAPER at the Asia Pacific Marketing Conference held in Malaysia. He is also a reviewer to several international journals having a high impact factor. He is the guide for M. Phil and PhD students of several universities in India. More than 100 research scholars have received their PhD and M. Phil degree under his guidance. He is also the author of several books and is the Chief Editor to several national and international journals of repute. Additionally, he has written several books on Management which have been highly received by the student and corporate community. He is also advisor to several Management colleges in and around Mumbai. He is also Independent Director on Board of several startups and MSME's

Prof. Dr. R. Gopal is the recipient of the RASHTRIYA VIDYA SARASWATI PURASKAR awarded by the International Institute of Education and Management. RASHTRIYA VIKAS

RATAN AWARD, awarded by the Economic Growth Society of India, Glory of India Award awarded by the Indo British Society, London, Rajiv Gandhi Education Excellence Award

BEST TEACHER AWARD awarded by the Higher Education Forum. BEST MANAGEMENT TEACHER AWARD in Management Education by the MTC Global and Knowledge Café, Educationist Award by the National and International Compendium, New Delhi. Prof. Dr. R. Gopal received Distinguished Service Award 2022 from IIT Kharagpur – January 2023-It is awarded in recognition of exceptional and distinguished service and outstanding contribution to the progress of the Institute. STAR OF ASIA award and many many more.

Prof. Dr. Vani Kamath

Dr Vani Kamath is a distinguished finance faculty with more than 20 years of experience in the field of teaching, research and administration. She has completed PhD in Finance from D Y Patil Deemed To be University, MBA and BBM from Mangalore University with distinction. Higher Education Forum has awarded Best Teacher Award to her for her distinguished service in the area of finance. She is currently working as a Professor and Former Dean at D Y Patil Deemed To Be University School of Management. She has published more than 50 research papers in national and international journals indexed in Scopus and UGC Care. She has bagged several best research paper awards for her publications and presentations. She has successfully guided PhD students and three students are awarded PhD under her guidance. She is empaneled with Securities and Exchange Board of India as a Securities Market trainer and has been taking sessions in various institutes of repute and has received outstanding feedback in these institutes She has successfully completed the funded research project sponsored by BRIT (Board of Radiation and Isotope Technology). She is Proficient in Excel and financial modeling. She has conducted several training sessions in several academic institutes and corporates.

Dr. Priya Vij

Dr. Priya Vij in an Associate Professor at D Y Patil Deemed to be University School of Management (School of Arts and Commerce). She has having more than 20 years of experience in Industry and Academics. She was associated with IT giants like Accenture Services Private Limited, FISERV India, Nucleus Software exports limited. She has authored more than 30 Research publications in prestigious National and International Journals indexed in SCOPUS and UGC Care, contributing significantly to the field. She received the Best Research paper award in the International Research Conference2020 organized by Global Business School and Research center Pune. She has many Copyrights and patents in her name. She has authored books titled "Business Analytics: An Overview", "Concepts of AI", "Essentials of Healthcare Analytics" and "Introduction to Marketing Analytics". She expertise in teaching subjects: Business Analytics, Big data, MIS, Information System Concepts, Technology management, ERP, DBMS, Creativity and Innovation Management, Operating Systems and various IT related subjects

Preface

Financial analytics is a critical aspect of modern business decision-making, offering insights that help organizations and individuals understand their financial performance, forecast future trends, and make informed choices. By leveraging tools, techniques, and methodologies such as data analysis, statistical modeling, and advanced algorithms, financial analytics transforms raw financial data into actionable intelligence.

This field encompasses a wide range of activities, including financial planning, investment analysis, risk management, and performance evaluation. It involves examining historical financial data to identify patterns, understanding key performance indicators (KPIs), and projecting future outcomes. Financial analytics is not limited to corporate finance; it plays a pivotal role in areas like personal finance, market research, and economic policy development.

In recent years, advancements in technology, such as artificial intelligence, machine learning, and big data analytics, have revolutionized the field. These innovations enable real-time data processing, more accurate predictions, and enhanced decision-making capabilities. Financial analytics now often integrates with tools like dashboards, data visualization platforms, and cloud-based software to provide dynamic and accessible insights.

This book is useful for the business leader aiming to optimize profitability, an investor seeking to maximize returns, or a policymaker evaluating economic strategies, financial analytics serves as a foundational tool to navigate the complexities of financial decision-making.

Acknowledgement

Writing this book has been a journey of discovery, growth, and perseverance, and we are deeply indebted to those who supported us along the way.

First and foremost, our gratitude goes to the stalwarts of the industry, whose insights, encouragement, and expertise guided me through every stage of this book. Their feedback and suggestions have enriched this book immeasurably.

We would like to extend my heartfelt thanks to our family and friends for their unwavering support and understanding during the countless hours we devoted to this work. Their belief in us kept us motivated and inspired.

A special thanks to the editor, for their meticulous attention to detail and for helping shape our ideas into their final form. To the publisher, Notion Press, thank you for believing in this project and bringing it to life.

Finally, to the readers, thank you for choosing to embark on this journey with us. Your curiosity and engagement are the greatest reward of all.

This book is a testament to the collaborative spirit of everyone involved. We are profoundly grateful for the contributions, encouragement, and belief in this endeavor.

Foreword

In an era where data is often considered the king, financial analytics stands at the forefront of transforming raw data into actionable insights. The convergence of technology, big data, and advanced analytical techniques has revolutionized the way we understand and interact with financial markets, corporate finance, and economic trends.

Financial analytics is not merely a tool but a strategic necessity in today's complex and fast- paced financial environment. It empowers organizations to make informed decisions, identify trends, mitigate risks, and seize opportunities with unprecedented accuracy and speed. From investment banking and asset management to corporate finance and personal financial planning, the applications of financial analytics are vast and varied. To work in financial analytics, one needs robust technical skills that include financial modelling, valuation, analysis and forecasting. The careers available in this field include insurance companies, business media and private investment firms. The technical skills required by the professionals are valuation analysis, joint venture analysis, internal rate of return, return on investment capital, Net present value, financial modelling, corporate finance, merger and acquisition analysis, leveraged buyout etc. Hence it becomes imperative for the finance professionals to understand the intricacies of financial analytics through this book.

This book aims to provide a comprehensive guide to the principles, methodologies, and practical applications of financial analytics. Whether one is a seasoned finance professional, a data scientist stepping into the world of finance, or a student aspiring to build a career in this dynamic field, this text is designed to equip everyone with the knowledge and skills needed to excel.

Mr. Anant Singhania CEO
JK Enterprises

Industry Speaks

As a banker having worked across multiple institutions for around three decades, I am witness to the changes that our financial world has seen over last 2-3 decades as technology started making inroads into every aspect of our lives including financial markets/institutions. The advent of technology has revolutionized the financial sector. For banks, it started with simple automation from use of ALPMs (Automated Ledger Posting Machines) which facilitated the automation of basic function of posting of entries and maintenance of ledgers in banks. It progressed to use of core banking systems which transformed the whole of banking operations followed by online banking which added to the ease of banking through net-banking and mobile banking. The technology has made further inroads through digitization, RPA (Robotic Process Automations), blockchain, etc. Since the banking system is connected to the entire financial world, technology has pervaded every part of it adding ease to usage at every stage be it initiation of a transaction, processing or execution. With the advent of big data, the focus has tilted towards data analytics, machine learning, AI, etc.

When Prof. Dr. R Gopal approached me for writing the foreword, it brought a lot of excitement to me as the subject is very close to my heart and I have been actively part of the technological transformative journey in banking and financial markets for around three decades. Knowing

Prof. Dr. R Gopal personally as a meticulous analytical explorer who likes to go to the depths of the subject with sharp analytical focus, wide coverage and depth of each topic reflected in every chapter covered in this book though does not come as a surprise to me but would certainly be a delight for the reader. He and his co-authors with their decades of experience in the field bring enormous value for the reader.

Technological changes over the years have metamorphosed our lives by impacting almost every area in our life. From communications which has made it easy to connect all the time, added convenience through emails, phones, messaging, social media to healthcare where new devices and scans like USG and MRI have made detection and the extent of effect of an ailment much easier, use of new medical gadgets, patient record keeping, all have led to better patient care. Similarly, in the field of education online learning platforms, virtual classrooms, and interactive tools, have made learning more accessible even to people from remote areas. Business operations have also achieved significant efficiencies through use of technologies like automation, data analytics, e-commerce etc. Financial world being an inalienable part of business ecosystem could not have escaped this transformation. In fact, it has achieved a quantum jump in terms of growth, efficiency, speed, convenience and remarkable facilitation to business growth through use of new technologies.

As an active participant of the financial markets, I have been part of the transformation that it has undergone because of the new technologies that have influenced our lives. Online and mobile banking, which was unthinkable a few decades back, forms the basics of banking technology now. We would earlier see most of the customers as walk-ins at the branch which is reduced to the minimal mostly with ones who are either not users of mobile/online banking or have difficulty in use of technology – a minority in any case. Digitization has reduced paper- based working to the minimal. There has been an unimaginable growth of digital transactions over the last decade.

As per Reserve Bank of India, there has been a 90-fold growth in retail digital payments in India from FY2013 growing from 162 crore in 2013 to over 15, 000 crore in 2024. The growth necessitates data analysis for better understanding.

With finance forming an inseparable part of our lives, this book takes the reader to the realm of the financial world and the technological developments that form part of our financial world today. The book starts with clarity on key financial concepts to make it useful for non-finance reader/user as well. It also makes it easier for the user to relate to the technologies and their uses covered in subsequent chapters. It talks about the Business Analytics in detail highlighting the importance of it and how it benefits business across various activities. It goes on to cover the tools being used for business analytics and how they are benefitting us in number of ways. The description of concepts, tools and applications has been very appropriately used to give readers a complete idea about business analytics and how it helps to overcome challenges of the business. The coverage is exhaustive as it covers almost every aspect of business analytics and the tools and technologies available as on date. The authors have painstakingly taken efforts to cover the Computing Foundations in a detail way covering from data management to data storage, from data integration to ETL, from R to Python to Machine Learning. The book has not left any important tool or technique that has usage in financial analytics. It makes the book wholesome.

The book has covered tools like big data analytics, artificial intelligence, machine learning, data visualization, tools and techniques in financial analytics, predictive analytics etc quite exhaustively to give the reader a complete idea about these technologies and their applications across the financial world.

I feel the book is a must read for every finance enthusiast and even for professionals pursuing finance as technology is going to be a critical component of business/financial growth and the tools covered in the book would certainly help in enriching the reader with the concepts, usage and benefits of these techniques which one simply cannot escape in modern business world.

Mr. Jattindar Dassi Sr. Vice President II,
Treasury Operations HDFC Bank

Industry Speaks

With the rapid growth of the global economy and with the easy flow of information/data, it has become imperative to analyze the data blocks so that strategic decisions can be taken. Finance is a very important component not only of country specific economies but also of the global economy.

The book on financial analytics written by Prof. Dr. R. Gopal, Prof. Dr. Vani Kamath and Dr. Priya Vij delves into the technological world of financial analytics in a fairly detailed manner.

The book helps a financial manager in drawing customer insights understand areas of operational/inefficiencies career competitive analysis, Risk analysis, financial forecasting etc. The book explains fairly detailed and lucid manner. The various concepts of financial Analytics such as data visualization, Application of Digital data for managerial decision making, Introduction to AI, machine learning etc. are a treat to read. The chapters on descriptive analytics using trend analytics financial ratios, predictive analytics using regression analytics and time series analytics, Prescriptive analytics using scenario analytics and optimization models and financial modelling is an eye opener to any reader.

I feel that the book is a must read for every finance professional interested in his growth and career prospects. I would strongly recommend the book to universities and colleges so that students and also to every corporate financial analyst interested in finance as career can get substantial advantage of the same.

Mr. Santosh Jadhav Data Scientist
MoneyGram International

Industry Speaks

If data is the new gold in today's world, then data analysts are the miners and craftsmen who unlock its value, with technology serving as their essential tool. Financial analytics, in particular, is a field everyone should be familiar with. In a time when the opportunities for investing money have expanded, so too have the associated risks. Understanding the dynamics of financial analytics is crucial for making informed and precise decisions.

The author, through the book *"Financial Analytics - An Overview,"* seeks to demystify these concepts in a straightforward and accessible way, using real-world examples, charts, and diagrams. Recognizing that our lives are increasingly intertwined with technology, the author also explains the roles of Artificial Intelligence and Machine Learning in financial analytics in a manner that is easy to grasp.

In addition, the book delves into the future and emerging trends in the financial analytics world. It explores how evolving technologies, such as predictive analytics, and big data, are set to reshape the financial landscape. The author provides insights into how these advancements will impact decision-making processes, risk management, and investment strategies. By highlighting these future trends, the book equips readers with a forward-looking perspective, helping them stay ahead in a rapidly changing financial environment.

I highly recommend this book for both educational purposes and as a valuable reference in your office library. It's also an excellent resource for families managing household finances, offering insights into essential concepts like the "time value of money" and "personal finance." Moreover, I believe this book should be part of every school and college curriculum, introducing young minds to the world of finance early on.

Mr. Kumar Ramakrishnan
Executive Director for a leading Financial services group in Asia and over 30 years of experience in the Financial Services Industry

Chapter 1

Finance Foundation for Analytics

1.1 What is Finance?

Finance can be defined as the art and science of managing money. The major areas of finance are:

1. Financial services and

2. Managerial Finance or Corporate Finance.

Financial services involve the design and delivery of financial products to individual businesses and governments and it involves dealing with banks, institutions, investments, real estate, insurance etc.

Financial Management on the other hand is concerned with the duties and the responsibilities of the Finance Manager of the firm. The Finance managers are actively involved in the management of financial affairs of any type of business which could include private, public large or small profit seeking or not for profit businesses, etc. The job involves budgeting, financial forecasting, cash management, loan, capital, credit Management, investment analysis, funds Management etc. Considering the changing regulatory, economic environment coupled with globalization of business activities, and the uncertainties in the market place, the importance of financial management has increased by leaps and bounds.

As a Financial Analytics personnel, it is important to understand the various aspects of financial management so as to take the right decision. Some of the decision areas which every finance personnel must be aware of are investment analysis, working capital management, source of funds, cost of funds, determination of capital structure, dividend policy, risk and returns analysis etc. All these decision areas impact the objectives of the shareholders viz. wealth maximization.

1.2 Decision Areas in Finance

A brief about some of the important decision areas are given below

i. FINANCIAL STATEMENT ANALYSIS

This involves:

- Study of income statement

- Study of revenue, expenses and profitability

- Balance sheet Analysis – Study of Assets, liabilities and equities

- Cash flow Analysis- Study of cash inflows and outflows etc.

Ratio analysis is a very important tool in analysing financial statements. Generally, one does an interfirm comparison and intrafirm comparison of the ratios. The interfirm comparison helps in benchmarking the performance of the firm while the intrafirm comparison helps in studying the growth patterns and identifies weaknesses in the same.

Ratios are generally classified as liquidity ratios, capital structure ratios, profitability ratios, activity ratios etc.

Some of the important ratios which are widely used in the business analytics are:

$$1.\text{Current Ratios (C/R)} = \frac{\text{Current Assets}}{\text{Current Liablities}}$$

$$2.\text{ Inventory Turnover Ratio (ITOR)} = \frac{\text{Cost of Goods/Sales}}{\text{Average Inventory}}$$

Average Inventory = Opening Stock + Closing Stock/2

3. Debtors Turnover Ratio (DTOR) $= \dfrac{\text{Net Annual credit sales}}{\text{Average Debtors}}$

4. Gross Profit Ratio (G/PRatio) = Gross Profit/Sales*100

5. Operating Profit Ratio $= \left(\dfrac{\text{Operating cost}}{\text{Net sales}} \right) 100$

6. Debt/Equity Ratio (D/E) $= \dfrac{\text{outsiders fund}}{\text{shareholders fund}}$

7. Interest Coverage Ratio $= \dfrac{\text{Earning before interest and tax(EBIT)}}{\text{Interest Charges}}$

8. Capital Gearing Ratio $= \dfrac{\text{Common stock holer's equity}}{\text{fixed interest bearing funds}}$

9. Earnings per share (EPS) $=\text{NPAT} \dfrac{-\text{Preference Dividend}}{\text{No. of Equity Shares}}$

10. Price Earning Ratio (P/E Ratio) $= \dfrac{-\text{Marketing Value of Share}}{\text{Earning per share}}$

11. Net profit to Net worth Ratio

(N/P to N/W Ratio) $= \dfrac{\text{N/P}}{\text{Net Worth}} \times 100$

The study of ratio analysis also helps in evaluating the marketing strategy adopted by the firm. The study of the balance sheet helps in identifying the creditworthiness of an organization. Thus, a high debtor value could indicate inefficient collection from the customers or the creditors. This could trigger a look at the customer's credit policy.

Additionally, a higher value of debt could result in paying high level of interest on the loan taken. This interest has to be then recovered from the customers which could result in an increase in the cost of the product and hence the price and thus possibly making the product uncompetitive.

For the success of the organisation the firm should have a sustainable competitive advantage. Competitive advantage can occur due to some of the marketing strategies adopted by the firm. This advantage helps the firm in the short run. In the long run (more than 5 years) the firm must have a sustainable competitive advantage and this can be obtained by innovations in the product and with a greater emphasis or research and development cell. A sustainable competitive advantage creates a superior value to its customer compared to its rivals. This value can be defined as:

$$Value = \frac{Benefit(B)}{Price(P)} \, ratio$$

Benefit can be defined as the utility of the product to the customer while price is defined as the amount that the customer pays for the product. The objective of any firm should be always to increase this value high so that competitors cannot penetrate the gap. The price of the product is always given by formula

$$\textbf{Selling price = Cost price + Profit}$$

The value gap can be increased by developing new products and services.

ii. TIME VALUE OF MONEY

Time value of money is the important concept in taking financial discussions. This is because wealth Maximization is one of the very important objectives of financial management. Time Management of money recognizes the time of investment and the time when the profit is available. Funds have to be obtained today and spent today while the profits would be available perhaps after 2 to 3 years.

In order to understand the time value of money one needs to understand the compound Annual Interest formula which is

$$A = p\left(1 + \frac{r}{100}\right)^n$$

Where, A = Final amount received after certain period of time

P = The Principal amount invested initially

r = Rate of Interest

n = Number of periods

This means that an amount of Rs. 100 invested today would yield an amount of Rs 105 assuming an interest ratio of 5% pa. after one year, Rs. 110.25 after two years, Rs.115.76 after three years and so on.

Consequently, it means that Rs. 115.76 received 3 years later is equivalent to Rs.100 today at 5% interest.

This compounding technique forms the basis of any evaluation of a project. The value of any asset/security is thus the discounted value of all future cash flows associated with the relevant/ specified period.

This can be written as:

$$v = \frac{A_1}{(1+k)^1} + \frac{A_2}{(1+k)^2} + \cdots \frac{A_n}{(1+k)^n}$$

Where,

V= Value of the asset/security at time zero (+=0)

A= Cash flows streams expected at the end of year

k= Appropriate required/capitalization/discount rate or cost of capital

On a similar line valuation bonds/debenture, shares etc can be done.

iii. COST OF CAPITAL

Cost of capital is another very important tool that is used widely by corporates in evaluating the various projects that they implement. In the time value of money concept explained above corporates use this Cost of Capital as the interest rate- r.

Cost of Capital can be defined as the minimum rate of return that the firm must earn on its investment so that the value of the firm remains unchanged. It must be mentioned that corporates normally use the cost of capital as the basis for discounting the future profits/cash.

The cost of capital is also called as the discount rate that is used to determine the present value of the future earnings. The cost of capital is visualized and is composed of several elements. It is computed for each component of the capital (Equity, shareholders, preference shares, long term borrowings etc.). By combining the cost of each component of the capital one can derive the weighted average cost of capital – also called as composite cost of capital or the combined cost of capital.

Many a times corporates also increase this cost of Capital by some percentage so as to coverup the financial risk and or the business risk parameters. Corporates also use the term opportunity cost or implicit cost of capital and this can be defined as the rate of return associated with the best investment opportunity that the firm and its shareholders would have foregone if the present projects were considered instead of other projects.

iv. RISK AND RETURN

Risk can be defined as variation between the actual Rate of Return and the expected rate of return associated with the given asset while return rate is defined as the actual income received. Risk and Return is also another important topic for the financial Analyst. The Risk Return Analysis would cover areas related to single security or asset portfolios.

Risk can be measured from behavioural point of view and quantitative / statistical point of view. Behavioural risk can be measured through a technique called as sensitivity analysis while the use of standard deviation and coefficient of variation helps in measuring the quantitative / statistical measurement.

v. Risk and Return of Portfolios

Portfolio can be defined as a combination of two or more assets. Each portfolio has a risk return characteristic which maybe unique. Additionally, there could be an interplay between the various assets within a portfolio or between two or more portfolios.

Analysis of Risk vs Return for a portfolio for a given set of portfolios can be then analyzed so as to evolve an optimal set of portfolios.

As mentioned above risk can be also defined as the variability between the actual returns in relation to the expected returns. Some of the tools available to measure this variability are:

a)   Sensitivity analysis

b)   Scenario Analysis and

c)   Simulation Analysis

Financial Model for sensitivity analysis:

Illustration: Build A Sensitivity Analysis of gross profit for revenue growth and % of sales of margin

The revenue, costs and growth figures are given as follows:

	A08	A09
Revenues	1000	1150
% Growth		*15%*
Costs	700	805
Cost Margins	*70%*	*70%*
Gross Profit	300	345

The sensitivity analysis model can be built up as follows:

Revenue Growth (X axis) Cost Margin (Y axis)

345	-5.0%	0.0%	5.0%	10.0%	15.0%	20.0%	25.0%	30.0%
35.0%	617.50	650.00	682.50	715.00	747.50	780.00	812.50	845.00
40.0%	570.00	600.00	630.00	660.00	690.00	720.00	750.00	780.00
45.0%	522.50	550.00	577.50	605.00	632.50	660.00	687.50	715.00
50.0%	475.00	500.00	525.00	550.00	575.00	600.00	625.00	650.00
55.0%	427.50	450.00	472.50	495.00	517.50	540.00	562.50	585.00
60.0%	380.00	400.00	420.00	440.00	460.00	480.00	500.00	520.00
65.0%	332.50	350.00	367.50	385.00	402.50	420.00	437.50	455.00
70.0%	285.00	300.00	315.00	330.00	345.00	360.00	375.00	390.00
75.0%	237.50	250.00	262.50	275.00	287.50	300.00	312.50	325.00
80.0%	190.00	200.00	210.00	220.00	230.00	240.00	250.00	260.00
85.0%	142.50	150.00	157.50	165.00	172.50	180.00	187.50	195.00
90.0%	95.00	100.00	105.00	110.00	115.00	120.00	125.00	130.00

1. Steps in building the sensitivity analysis model:

2. Calculate gross profit for A08. Formula: Revenues-Cost = Gross Profit

3. Assume 15% growth in Revenues for A09.

4. The revenue is calculated as ₹1150

5. The cost margin is assumed as 70%

6. The cost works out as ₹805

7. Calculate gross profit for A09= ₹345

8. Prepare the table in excel with various hypothetical percentages of revenue growth on X axis and cost margin on Y axis.

9. Place the cursor on the top left corner and link it with the gross profit figure of A09 i.e., 345

10. Drag the cursor from the first to the last row and last column.

11. Click on Data, What if analysis, Data Table, row input cell value (place the cursor at 15% of the table) and column input cell value (place the cursor at 70% of the table)

12. The forecasted values would appear in the blank spaces.

The accuracy can be checked by linking the revenue growth percentage (15%) with the cost margin (70%) of A09

Financial Model for scenario analysis:

Illustration:

Build a financial model for a company for 3 years with three scenarios.

   a) Best Case

   b) Base Case and

   c) Worst Case

The revenue and cost scenarios are all the 3 years are given below. The revenues, cost and net income for 3 years needs to be calculated in the first part of the table.

1. Methods for calculation:

2. Click on the cell below 1-1-2022

3. Use the formula Choose

4. Take the cursor to 1 for index number

5. Scroll the cursor down for the values of Best, base and worst case for the year 1-1-22

6. The blank columns for the year 2022 would appear.

7. The same formula can be dragged for rest of the two years to get the values.

8. The choose value 1 can be changed to 2 and 3 to get the values for all the 3 scenarios.

Rs in actual figures	01-01-2022	01-01-2023	01-01-2024
Revenues	50000	125000	250000
Cost	-5000	-12500	-25000
Net Income	45000	112500	225000
Choose Scenario 1			
Revenue Scenarios Best Case	50000	125000	250000
Base Case	25000	37500	50000
Worst Case	12500	13000	13250
Cost Scenarios Best Case	-5000	-12500	-25000
Base Case	-16000	-25000	-37500
Worst Case	-22500	-30000	-45000

Risk can be evaluated using the following methods:

1. Risk adjusted discount rate

2. Certainty Equal Approach

3. Probability distribution approval and

4. Decision tree approach

v. EVALUATION OF INVESTMENT

Investment:

Investment can be defined in many different ways. It can be defined as an advance payment of money to some other person (E.g. loan to another person) for a return. Or when a person invests money in the purchase of gold and jewellery or in some services like insurance policy or in some shares, bonds etc.

The objective of any investor is generally

a)   Income

b)   Capital Appreciation

c)   Safety

d)   Liquidity or

e)   Hedge against inflation

The fund that can be invested for a short period less than or equal to 1 year. It is called short term fund. The periods which are more than 1 year are called long term.

EVALUATION OF INVESTMENT PROPOSALS

Investments are generally evaluated by the following methods:

a)   Urgency Method

b)   Payback Period method

c)   Unadjusted Return on Investment Method or Average Rate of Return Method (ARR)

d) Net Present Value Method

e) Internal Rate of Return Method

f) Terminal Value Method

g) Benefit Cost Ratio Method

a) Urgency Method

In many situations in the life of a business concern an ad hoc decision is needed with respect of an investment expenditure. For instance, if a part of the machine stops working leading to complete breakdown and disruption in the production process, it would be justified to replace it immediately by a new one even without comparing the cost and future profit. Any decision on investment expenditure on the basis of urgency should be taken only if it is fully warranted and justified.

b) Pay-Back Period Method

This is also known as 'payoff and pay out' method. This method is employed to determine the number of years required for the capital expenditure incurred to pay for itself. The Payoff is the method described in terms of period of time (e.g. in years).

The pay-back period is the number of years required to recover the investment. The criterion is that the average income from a proposed investment is sufficient to cover investment within a period of time. It is calculated:

$$\text{Pay-back period} = \frac{\text{Investment}}{\text{Income/year}}$$

Normally the return is calculated on an after-tax basis but before depreciation.

c) Average Rate of Return Method (ARR)

This method is also called Accounting Rate of Return Method or Financial Statement Method on Return on Investment or Average Rate of Return Method. Here the main feature is that the rate of return is based on the figures for income and investment which are determined according to conventional accounting concepts.

The rate of return is expressed as a percentage of the earnings to the investment in a particular project. Income may be taken as the average annual earnings, normal earnings or the earnings of the first year of the project. Investments may be taken as the initial investment or the average outlay over the life of the investment.

The rate of return on investment refers to the rate of interest that will make the present value of future earnings just equal to the cost of investment.

It may be calculated as following:

d) Net Present Value

The net present value method is one of the discounted cash flow or time adjusted method. This is generally considered to be the best method for evaluating capital investment proposals. In case of this method, cash inflows and cash outflows associated with each project are first worked out.

The net present value is the difference between the total present value of future cash inflows and the total present value of future cash outflows. The equation for calculating net profit value in case of conventional cash flows can be as follows:

$$NPV = \left(\frac{R_1}{(1+k)^1} + \frac{R_2}{(1+k)^2} + \cdots \frac{R_n}{(1+k)^n} + \cdots \right) - 1$$

where NPV = Net present value

R = Cash inflows at different time periods k = Cost of capital

I = Cash outflows

e) Internal Rate of Return Method

This method is also called Time Adjusted Return on Investment or Discounted Rate of Return. This method measures the rate of return which earnings are expected to yield on investments. Internal rate of return is defined as the maximum rate of interest that could be paid for the capital employed over the life of an investment without loss on the projects.

The rate is similar to the effective rate of interest calculated on debentures purchased or sold. This is calculated on the basis of the funds utilised from time to time as opposed to the investment made at the beginning. This method incorporates the time value of money in the investment calculation.

The formula for the discounted rate of return is

$$C = \left[\frac{F_1}{(1+r)^1} + \frac{F_2}{(1+r)^2} + \cdots \frac{F_3}{(1+r)^3} + \cdots + \frac{S_n}{(1+r)^n} \right]$$

C = the supply price of the asset.

F = the future cash flows.

S = the salvage value of the asset in years,

r = the discounted rate of return.

f) Terminal Value Method

This method is based on the assumption that operating saving of each year is invested in another outlet at a certain rate of return from the moment of its receipt till the end of the economic life of the projects. This method incorporates the assumption about how the cash inflows are reinvested once they are received and thus avoids any influence of the cost of capital on cash inflows. However, cash inflows of the last year of the project will not be reinvested.

The compounded values of cash inflows should be determined as the basis of compounding factor which may be obtained from compound interest table or by the following formula:

$$A = P(1+i)\ n \text{ where } P=1$$

g) Benefit-Cost Ratio Method

This method is based on time adjusted techniques and is also called Profitability Index or Desirability Factor. The procedure of deriving the benefit cost ratio criterion is the same as that of NPV. In this cost the present value of the benefit is divided by the present value of the cost. The ratio between the two would give us the benefit-cost ratio which indicates benefit per rupee of cost.

The calculation of benefit-cost ratio is shown as follows

$$\text{Benefit Cost Ratio (BCR)} = \frac{\text{Present value of Benefits}}{\text{Present value of Cost}}$$

vi. CAPITAL BUDGETING

Capital Budgeting refers to assets which are in operation and yield return over a period of time. Link to capital budgeting is a term commonly referred as capital expenditure. Capital Expenditure are normally spread over a period of time. Capital budgeting decisions are of paramount importance in financial decision making. These decisions have a tremendous bearing on the profitability of the firm. They also have a bearing the competitive position of the firm. Capital budgeting in fact enables through the manufacturing processes is likely to yield profits.

The evaluation of Capital budgets could impact:

- Investment decisions which affect the revenue

- Investment decisions which affect the cost

The evaluation process could result in

1. An accept-reject decision

2. Accept-reject decision for mutually exclusive projects and

3. Capital rationing decisions

In order to prepare capital budget several financial factors are involved. Typically, cash flow details, Tax details, depreciation details, direct and indirect cost effect on other projects etc. The tool that are use are essentially net present value (NPV), internal/rate of return (IRR) average rate of return (ARR) and profitability index. In evaluating capital budgets care must be taken to consider the impact of inflation.

There are different types of budget in addition to capital budgets. Some of them are:

1. Operating budgets (Sales budget, Production budget, direct labour budget, manufacturing expenses budget and administrative and selling expenses budget)

2. Financial budget (Income statement, retained earning statements, cash budget, budgeted balance sheet)

The starting point for any budgeting is the sales budget. The sales budget gives the total revenue that will be earned by the firm. Cash budget is one of the most important budgets. This budget helps in meeting payment schedule, minimizing funds, outflow related to cash balances. It provides an overview of the requirement of cash during the various time periods. The cash budget helps the financial analyst to identify Time periods where the requirement of cash is maximum and perhaps needs to be supplemented to borrowings or other means.

vii. EVALUATION OF PROJECTS

Corporates normally prepare a feasibility report for evaluation of large projects involving a number of years/large investments. This feasibility report is also called as a business plan or Techno- economic feasibility report (TEFR) and forms the basis for any investments evaluating correct amount made by banks, venture capitalist etc., It normally comprises of two parts

a) Industry Analysis and

b) Financial Analysis

The business plan generally covers the following aspects:

i. Executive Summary (giving a brief overview of the project etc.)

ii. Company Description

iii. Products and Services (referred and proposal)

iv. Market Characteristics

v. Marketing Plan (in brief)

vi. Manufacturing Process including a brief on the raw materials, personnel required etc.

vii. Operational Plan

viii. Management and Organization

ix. Startup Expenses and Capitalization

x. Financial Plan including profit and Loss account, Capital Structure analysis, Depreciation plan, Cash flow analysis, Ratio analysis, Break even Analysis, IRR etc.

viii.   BEHAVIOURAL FINANCE

Many a times it is observed that investors especially in the stock markets invest based upon emotional criterias rather than logic and rational criteria. Behavioural finance tries to study this aspect of investment decisions.

Behavioural finance can be defined as an economic theory that explains many a times the irrational financial behaviour for e.g. over spending on credit cost, panic selling of stocks during a market downtown. Some of the issues involved are:

a)   Financial psychology

b)   Herd Mentality

c)   Loss aversion

d)   Heuristic (i.e. simplifying the problem when sufficient and enough information is not available to make a perfect decision)

e)   Mental accounting (i.e. blowing of windfall many on a spontaneous shopping while in a normal case all spending are carefully planned.

The biggest advantage of understanding behavior finance is that it helps in understanding the impact of such decisions on the portfolio management.

ix. PORTFOLIO MANAGEMENT

Portfolio management involves the strategic management of a group of investments e.g. wide range of assets like stocks, bonds, real estate etc. The main goal of portfolio management is to optimize the returns and control the risk involved based upon the investors, time horizon, goals, risk tolerance etc

x. FINANCIAL MODELLING

Financial modelling is the process of developing models to depict the performance of a firm asset or a project. These models are used to evaluate risk to predict the future and assist in decision making. Some of the applications are in the areas of Equity research, Initial public offerings (IPO), forecasting and budgeting, sensitivity analysis, scenario analysis etc. Excel application, Monte Carlo modelling are widely used in finance modelling. Financing modelling is also used in evaluating of projects and in predicting future trends in business.

Chapter 2

Harnessing Big Data in Finance

2.1 Introduction

In today's fast-moving, interconnected world, data has turned out to be a very valuable asset for organizations in many diverse industries, mostly in finance. The ability to analyze copious volumes of information can thus be quite helpful for good risk management, decision-making, and customer interaction. A better understanding is needed of Big Data and Financial Analytics regarding their definition and importance, relation, and applications in the financial sector.

2.2 Definition of Big Data

Big Data is the colossal volumes of data-structured, semi-structured, and unstructured-that are produced at an unprecedented rate from diverse sources. It is described by what has been termed the "3 Vs," referring to the three prime features of the data in question.

Volume: This is used to describe the enormous volume of data produced every single day- terabytes and petabytes, if one wants to get technical. This would include everything from social media interactions to bank transaction data.

Velocity: The speed of generation and processing means that financial markets' movements and fraud detection should be analysed in real time.

Variety: The type of data ranges from unstructured data to conventional structured data, including emails, photos, and posts on social media down to transaction records. It is to be expected that from the data collected, much insight will come through advanced analytics.

Big data is the backbone of modern society, as practically everything moves on data. Big data for business purposes includes enhancing customer experiences, managing risks, optimizing operations, and extracting knowledge about customer behaviour. Its transformative potential allows businesses to make decisions using data, becoming more innovative and competitive in a rapidly changing environment.

2.3 Characteristics of Big Data

The features of Big Data have to be known for harnessing its potential in diversified ranges of sectors, specifically financial analytics. Big data can often be defined by the "5 Vs" that amply describe the distinctive features of big data.

The 5 Vs of Big Data

Volume: Size and Scale of Data

Volume defines the vast amount of data being generated and collected. Examples of these are financial transaction records, market data, social media interactions, and customer data that can add up to several terabytes or petabytes of data. The volume is enormous; such an enormous amount of data produces difficulties in its processing, management, and storage. Such huge volumes may be beyond the capacity of traditional databases, hence the need for cloud-based systems and distributed storage options. When this volume is managed, organizations can delve deep into the analyses and gain greater insights.

Velocity: The Speed of Data Generation and Processing

Velocity refers to the speed of creation, gathering, and analysing information. Real-time data flows come to the finance industry through a host of sources, including social media, online transactions, and stock exchanges. While a rapid generation of data is required, processing and analysis are also required instantly for timely decision-making. For example, real-time analytics on fraudulent activity can be recognized at the actual time it occurs for businesses to minimize such risks immediately. The ability to handle high-velocity data streams helps in the competitive level within the financial sector.

Variety: Different Forms and Sources of Data

Variety is the huge diversity in the type of data that organizations deal with. Big Data also encompasses different data types such as unstructured data in the form of text documents, images, and posts on social networking sites. Moreover, big data also includes semi-structured data in the forms of XML and JSON, and structured data in the form of numerical data kept in databases. Examples of different types of data sources for finance include transactional data, market data, consumer behaviour data, and external factors like economic indicators. Such diversity in sources of data does indeed call for advanced methods and tools for analysis to integrate, process, and make sense of the data.

Veracity: Reliability and Accuracy of Data

Veracity refers to the quality and reliability of the data. For the large amounts of data that are being made available at one's fingertips, the ability to ensure consistency in the level of accuracy will be fundamental to making trustworthy decisions. Reputational risks, weak financial analysis, and poor investment strategies result from inaccurate or unreliable data. Data governance procedures and validation procedures that are strictly followed through represent the only ways financial institutions can be sure that the analyzed data is accurate. Indeed, for the insights to be reliable, there needs to be a great deal of data cleansing and validation.

Value: Insights and Benefits Derived from Data

Value is derived from the insights and benefits there are to organizations in analysing volumes of data. The ability to transform unstructured data into meaningful insights that drive decision- making is the ultimate goal in the use of big data. It can be in terms of delivering investment opportunities, enhancing risk management strategies, increasing customer delight, or improving overall operational efficiency within the financial system. Innovation and competitive advantage in the financial services are Segwayed through and by the ability of one to extract insightful information from the data.

Other Characteristics

In addition to these five characteristics, two other imperative features come into consideration, namely complexity and timeliness.

Complexity

Complexity defines Big Data in terms of its intricacy and the challenges that are brought forth in manipulating and making something useful out of it. The data ecosystem out of many instances consists of numerous different formats, sources, and varied systems of storage, hence developing intricate relationships between data points. The integration of data in finance from various transaction systems, customer databases, and external market feeds can be a very challenging issue. For this reason, there arises a massive need for modern and sophisticated means of data integration, equally intelligent analytics, and professionals capable of traversing the complex landscape of data in an attempt to source out meaningful insights.

Timeliness

Timeliness is one of the essential qualities for big data, especially in fast-paced activities such as finance. Success in decision-making relies on the capability of evaluating information and making corresponding decisions as quickly as possible. All financial markets are fluid; everything is dynamic and always changing. Companies will be better positioned to react to shifting consumer needs, changes in the market, and newly emerging threats when relevant information is provided in a timely way. Real-time analytics and monitoring solutions have been enabling banking institutions to be competitive and have created more room for agility and responsiveness.

Each of the five Vs-pointing toward volume, velocity, variety, veracity, and value-add timeliness and complexity-provides special opportunities and challenges in handling enormous datasets. Timely, accurate data analysis at both the macro and granular levels can drive key shifts in strategic decision-making for the financial industry, benefiting from Big Data more than most industries.

2.4 Big Data: Importance in Finance

Big data nowadays has become an important enabler in the financial industry to serve various organizations better for the purpose of raising customer service, making decisions, and operating their operations. By utilizing large data sets, organizations can unlock insights that drive innovation and competitive advantage.

Transformation of Financial Services:

Big data has indeed changed the financial services landscape today with its profound impacts on how customers are engaged, what services are offered, and how operations are performed.

Operational Changes:

The flow of information made the financial organizations think in terms of their operating model. Many technologies using machine learning and artificial intelligence replace the conventional procedures of data management and analysis. Such technologies, for example, critically help the smooth compliance functions, enhance risk management and make it possible to execute many routine tasks which are time consuming, thus making organizations leaner and reducing operational costs.

Services:

Big Data has brought huge diversity in services provided by financial institutions. Today, it is possible to produce financial products especially tailor-made to the needs of every particular customer. Today, for example, a bank uses predictive analytics to present loan proposals individually and unique for each customer, in line with their history of transactions and financial behaviour. Among these business models are peer-to-peer lending, roto-advisors, and mobile banking applications, the possibility of which Big Data integration may provide.

Customer Engagement:

Big data enables financial institutions to get a deeper insight into their customers and thus, serve them better. Organizations can employ big data analytics to tap into customers' pain areas and create customized marketing strategies that boost customer happiness and loyalty. Real-time analytics further enhances experience as consumer queries can be replied quickly.

Smarter Decision Making:

The most important implication that Big Data brings to finance today is a shift toward data-driven decision-making. Soon, data analytics will be one of the major tools financial organizations will make strategic and operational choices with.

Data-Driven Strategies:

Putting big data enables financial institutions in better decisions rather than intuition. For example, predictive modelling helps an investment business know what is going on in the market. It also leads to better portfolio performance with optimum investment methods. Such data-driven initiatives can help raise returns and optimize resources, providing superior risk assessments for an institution.

Risk management:

Big data can be used to assist with decision-making. Institutions have to analyze large datasets for the prediction and development of mitigations against possible risks. Advanced analytics point out potential fraud and allow preventive measures to block further financial loss by pointing out anomalies in data transactions.

Regulatory Compliance:

Data analytics is being put to use for adapting to ever-evolving regulations. Big Data allows banks and other financial institutions to track transactions in real time and thus detect potential areas of non-compliance. With this approach, such institutions will thus be able to avoid committing non-compliance with any regulatory prescriptions. Such an approach therefore lowers the chances of having fines associated with noncompliance and encourages a culture of being transparent and responsible. Its importance in finance cannot be exaggerated. It has revolutionized financial services through improvements in operations, the facilitation of data-driven decisions, and service personalization. As the financial world continues to evolve, success and innovation will still heavily depend on the strategic application of big data.

2.5 Sources of Big Data in Finance

The sources of big data in finance are several and varied; they also range from internal to external sources. Such an understanding of these sources is crucial for any financial institution that intends to use this data efficiently for analytics, risk management, and making decisions.

Internal Data Sources Transactional Data

Transactional data represents some of the most useful internal sources of Big Data in the finance industry. It contains the record of all transactions, including purchases, transfers, withdrawals, and deposits that a financial institution engages in. This information is important in analysing account activities for fraud detection and helps in understanding consumer behaviour. Through transactional data analysis, financial institutions can improve their efficiency in operations, optimize product offerings, and identify spending habits of customers. For example, through advanced analytics of transactional data, organizations get information that will inform strategies related to risk management and focused advertising campaigns.

Historical Financial Data

As the name would suggest, this broad class of data encompasses historical records of the performance of a financial organization. Such data would include balance sheets, cash flow statements, income statements, and past stock prices. Historical financial data analysis forms the basis of trend analysis, performance forecasting, and well-informed investment decisions. For example, considering historical financial performance, companies can find the relationship between different financial indicators and build predictive models that could assist them in future ways. Since it gives a history of financial activities and results over time, historical data is also extremely useful for regulatory compliance.

External Data Sources

Market Data: Stock Prices, Economic Indicators

Market data can be termed as one of the critical external sources of big data in finance. This stream of data contains the current bond yield, stock price, volume of trade, economic indicators like Gross Domestic Product, which is the growth rate of a country, unemployment rate, and inflation rate. It also includes all the above pieces of information that are vital for strategic decisions, risk analysis, and investment analysis. Market data allows financial institutions to gauge volatility in the market, locate avenues for investment, and arrive at well- informed decisions about trading. By monitoring economic indicators, organizations can estimate various macroeconomic trends that may affect their financial performance.

Customer Data: Surveys and Feedback

Information obtained about customers through surveys and feedback provides valuable inputs about customer preference, behavior, and satisfaction. Financial institutions conduct questionnaires among their customers to help them determine their feelings towards the services, products, and experiences associated with them. Through this information, analyzed for desired results, an organization can design targeted marketing campaigns, improve customer engagement, and take remedial action where necessary. In this respect, financial institutions can improve customer satisfaction and loyalty by designing their services to better match the needs and pain points of their customers.

Social Media Data

Presently, social media sites have emerged as a Big Data asset that can be used to draw inferences about market trends, consumer sentiment, and brand perception. Analyzing interaction on social media sites will help financial institutions to gauge the pulse of the general public on business initiatives, financial products, and economic events. By conducting sentiment analysis on social media information, companies can make more informed decisions about marketing based on actual data, thus enabling them to get a better view of consumer attitudes and preferences. In addition, monitoring social media conversations helps the financial institutions to align their approaches with the development of new trends and emergence of new risks.

IoT Data (Devices, Sensors)

The Internet of Things is slowly emerging as one of the gravest sources of financial Big Data. Wearables, smart home appliances, and connected cars are just a few examples that show IoT devices create enormous volumes of data obtainable for several financial uses. For instance, connected car data can be used by insurance companies to assess driving habits with increased precision for the determination of premiums. On the other hand, financial institutions can take leverage from IoT data by improving risk assessments, increase knowledge of their customers, and creating innovative products and services that align with consumer changing trends.

All the varied sources of Big Data in the industry-ranging from external to internal data sources such as market data, customer data, social media data, Internet of Things data, transactional data, and all forms of historical financial records-manage to enable financial institutions to compile a deluge of data that informs them in strategy and decision-making.

2.6 Big Data Applications in Financial Analytics

Financial analytics is one of the prime drivers in today's financial world. It allows every business to derive insight from data and make decisions based on those insights. Financial analytics allow an organization to realize the position of its finances, how resources can be allocated most effectively, and identify possibilities for growth and areas needing improvement.

Big Data analytics represent the full transformation of financial analytics to extract priceless insights from volumes and variety of data. Risk management, fraud detection, portfolio management, and client segmentation are some of the big data applications in financial analytics. Each one of them explains how a business benefits from using data in enhancing financial performances and decision-making procedures.

Risk Management

It includes identifying, measuring, and mitigating potential risks to the financial institution's operations and profits. Big Data analytics gives diverse insights from many datasets, identifying trends and projecting future dangers, allowing a financial institution to establish comprehensive risk management plans.

Identification of risks:

Financial analysts can utilize data analytics to identify new hazards that would not be detected using traditional techniques of research by combining information from numerous sources, such as economic indicators, market patterns, and previous experience. For example, an institution can easily monitor market movements and adapt accordingly using updated data analytics.

Fraud Detection

The various problems that fraud can bring upon financial institutions include large losses and damage to reputation. Accordingly, big data analytics deploys state-of-the-art techniques in the detection and prevention of fraud to support business in protecting their assets and ensuring continued customer confidence.

Fraud Detection Techniques:

Anomalies that could lead to fraudulent transactions are detected through analysing patterns of transactions with the use of algorithms in data mining and machine learning. Clustering algorithms may group similar transactions in a representative model of spending habits. For example, analysts can segregate unusual transactions from normal ones using a machine learning model.

Real-time Monitoring:

Analysing data at real time is of essence in fraud detection. The financial institutions can establish automated mechanisms that are always observing the transactions and trigger a red flag in case suspicious activities occur. Proactivity by the organizations reduces losses and minimizes the risks involved through quick response to fraudulent situations.

Analyzing Customer Behaviour

Transactional data analysis, customer interactions, and feedback will help financial institutions to identify discrete customer segments based on their behaviour and needs. The perception can be portrayed on data-driven insights such as spending trends, preferred channels of communication, and product preferences to help businesses customize their products appropriately.

Segmentation thus facilitates marketing directed at specific segments of the audience. Financial institutions can simply employ tailored promotions, marketing messaging, and product suggestions to appeal to a variety of client tastes. This method improves conversion rates and consumer engagement.

Portfolio Management

Portfolio management necessitates extensive understanding of market dynamics and investment performance. Big Data analytics enables financial experts to conduct detailed performance analysis and develop evidence-based investment strategies. Big Data enables portfolio managers to evaluate large amounts of market data based on past performance, economic indicators, and geopolitical events. This research assists the portfolio manager in identifying an investment opportunity and its associated risks, allowing them to make informed decisions about investment strategy and asset allocation.

Big data analytics enables the tracking and measurement of portfolio performance over time. Portfolio managers can monitor key performance indicators for various strategies and compare them to market indexes to determine how their strategies performed and make required modifications. A data-driven strategy improves investment portfolio management in general.

Big Data applications in financial analytics range from risk management and fraud detection to customer segmentation and portfolio management, demonstrating the industry's revolutionary capacity for insight-driven decisions. Leveraging Big Data allows financial businesses to improve operational efficiency, decision-making, and, ultimately, financial performance. As technology advances, it becomes increasingly important to include various advanced analytics approaches in order to remain competitive and address the demands of the financial landscape.

2.7 Big Data Challenges

Big Data presents both opportunities and challenges in finance, where vast volumes of data from trading, transactions, regulatory filings, social media, and economic indicators require advanced processing and analysis. A primary challenge is managing the *volume* of data generated daily, especially by high-frequency trading systems and global markets, which can overwhelm traditional data storage and processing systems. This vast amount of data must also be processed rapidly to support real-time decision-making, but the *velocity* of financial data streams can create bottlenecks and latency issues. Moreover, the *variety* of data ranging from structured transaction records to unstructured news articles and social media feeds requires complex integration and harmonization to ensure consistency and comparability across sources. *Veracity*, or data quality, is another significant challenge, as financial data is often noisy, incomplete, or biased, requiring rigorous data cleaning to maintain accuracy. Security and compliance are also critical concerns, as financial data often includes sensitive customer information and must adhere to stringent regulations, such as General Data Protection Regulation (GDPR) and Financial Industry Regulatory Authority (FINRA). To conclude, deriving actionable insights from Big Data requires sophisticated analytical tools, machine learning models, and skilled data scientists, making talent acquisition and technological investment additional challenges for financial institutions looking to leverage Big Data effectively.

2.8 Future Trends in Big Data and Financial Analytics

There are a host of trends that are emerging as financial institutions increasingly deploy Big Data analytics. The important future trends and how they impact financial analytics, starting with the role of AI and automation, real-time analytics, blockchain technology, and cloud computing.

AI and Automation in Finance

Artificial intelligence surely changes the face of financial analytics, developing its processing capabilities and allowing the conduction of more complex analyses. AI technologies become extremely helpful in making decisions on a wide range of financial assignments.

Real-Time Analytics

The real-time generation of insight becomes key in keeping one's competitive advantage in today's fast financial markets. Financial institutions should prepare themselves for quick responses to such situations as the market conditions are always fluctuating. Advanced analytics in real time help an organization stay on top of market trends, assess risks, and make well-informed decisions. Financial analysts have the ability to enhance trading activities by reaching quicker strategy adjustments and strengthening risk management procedures with real-time data feeds. Stream processing and in-memory computing are examples of technologies that will enable real-time analytics through the ability to process and analyze data as it is generated. That enables responsiveness and overall performance, whereby financial institutions now have the ability to act with speed in view of a new opportunity or threat.

Blockchain Technology

It holds immense power for blockchains to shift the way financial transactions and analytics are made. Blockchain has huge potential to bring greater transparency and reduce fraud, thereby making financial processes much more efficient. Blockchain technology can provide security in making transactions efficient through a reduction in the actual cost of transactions and the involvement of intermediaries. Blockchain provides a source of trusted, tamper-proof data for analytics that will enable enterprises to track audits, ownership of assets, and-with more accuracy-analyse patterns in transaction trends.

Smart contracts are a form of self-executing contracts whereby the contractual rules are hardcoded into the code itself. This further entails higher levels of operational efficiency where there is an avoidance of intermediaries to impede procedures or heighten the risk of human error.

Cloud Computing

Cloud computing changed the dimensionality in which financial organizations used to store and process their data. It is more flexible, scalable, and cost-effective. Thus, with ever-growing demand for Big Data analytics, cloud solutions in the financial sector become of much wider importance.

The benefits of cloud computing in data processing and storage include that it allows storage of massive volumes of data without necessarily having an expensive on-premise infrastructure. This scalability advantage is very useful for any financial institution, as it will be easy for them to increase and decrease their storage capacity according to the requirements. Cloud platforms securely enable teams to collaborate more effectively by providing safe remote access to data and analytics tools. Innovation is fostered, and decision-making is enhanced as cloud platforms build greater capabilities among financial analysts to share ideas and collaborate on projects.

The reason is that Big Data and financial analytics were set to radically change because of developments currently occurring in AI, real-time analytics, blockchain, and cloud computing. In addition, with such trends, the financial institutions become more capable to drive data- based decisions, have a check on operational effectiveness, and offer personal services to customers.

2.9 Conclusion

As mentioned, the realm of finance has come full circle with big data and financial analytics converging. The financial organizations can realize better decision-making, operational effectiveness, and customized services to their clients using big datasets and advanced analytical techniques.

These dimensions of volume, velocity, variety, veracity, and value make Big Data so critical to financial institutions in offering unparalleled insights into consumer behaviour, market dynamics, and operational performance. Financial analytics is important since it provides a variety of ways to manage risk, plan strategies, and evaluate performance using data-driven methods. Since the big shift from traditional analytics to Big Data analytics took place, organizations can now explore real-time insights and predictive capabilities that generate competitive advantage.

In the end, there are various opportunities for innovation and expansion into the financial sector based on big data and financial analytics mergers. If they are properly understood, together with the ability to adapt to the changing environment, these trends have the potential for turning data analytics into a source of informed strategic decisions, superior customer service, and competitiveness in markets. Interconnected technology and finance, eventually create new frontiers in the industry, apart from setting a basis in which financial institutions relate to their customers.

Chapter 3

Introduction to Financial Analytics

3.1 Emergence of the Fintech Industry

One of the innovations that has disrupted the financial markets the most is financial technology (fintech). Information technology, regulations, and the economy are its main drivers. The entire financial system underwent a change with the advent of fintech. Every nation's economy is seriously threatened by global disintermediation. With 145 crore people, India is renowned for its tremendous demographic dividend. Fintech facilitates corporate transactions and is essential to the nation's progress. The 2015 financial revolution brought about systemic change. Start- up enterprises can now progress to the new system of specialised and customised services by overcoming the obstacles posed by the existing system thanks to technical advancements in big data analytics, mobile devices, and infrastructure.

Financial Services and Banking sector of India is considered as one of the robust systems in the world. The conventional banking and financial services system has been supplanted by contemporary technology. The telecom sector's introduction of free data has taken India's financial sector to a new and varied level. In the modern day, technology and finance have grown intertwined.

In India, fintech companies are changing the face of financial services. India has risen to the second spot in the EY FinTech Adoption Index 2017, trailing only China in terms of the uptake of FinTech services across a variety of industry sectors. The payment, wealth management, lending, capital market, insurance services, and real options business models are the main topics of the literature that is now available on the topic of the overview of the fintech ecosystem in financial markets. Throughout all of these many business strategies, financial analytics is extensively utilised.

3.2 Introduction to Finance

Finance encompasses a wide range of activities, including borrowing, lending, investing, budgeting, and managing risks. It is all about making decisions about how to allocate resources—whether it's individuals managing their personal finances, businesses raising capital for expansion, or governments planning their budgets. There are several branches of finance, each focusing on different aspects of the financial system. For example, corporate finance deals with the financial decisions made by companies, such as raising capital, investing in projects, and managing cash flow. There is also public finance, which handles taxation, budgeting, and public spending as well as the financial administration of governments and public institutions. In both the personal and professional spheres of life, finance is vital. It has an impact on nearly every facet of our lives, from the daily financial decisions we make to the more significant economic choices made by businesses and governments. The way we approach and think about financial issues is always changing due to new laws, regulations, and economic trends.

3.3 Introduction to Analytics

The methodical analysis of data or information and using this analysis to predict the future is referred to as analytics. It entails processing and interpreting data using a variety of methods and instruments. Analyzing data involves more than just looking at numbers or information; it involves using computational, mathematical, or statistical techniques. Data analysis allows for the discovery of hidden correlations, linkages, and patterns that might not be immediately apparent. This enables one to act on the basis of evidence rather than just instinct and make better informed decisions.

Analytics has numerous applications in a wide range of industries. Analytics, for example, can be used in finance to assess financial performance, optimize investments, and manage risks. The potential to use analytics to tackle challenging issues and spur innovation is only growing as technology develops.

3.4 Financial Analytics

Financial analytics is essentially the process of using data analysis techniques to understand financial trends, risks, and opportunities. Financial analytics would involve collecting and analyzing data on things like sales revenue, expenses, market trends, and economic indicators. For instance, one might use statistical methods to identify patterns or correlations in the data, or employ machine learning algorithms to predict future trends or outcomes. It can help understand which areas of the business is performing well and which might need improvement.

3.5 Difference Between Financial Analysis and Analytics

Financial analytics and financial analysis are very different from one another. Comparative statements, common size statements, trend analysis, ratio analysis, and cash flow statement analysis are among the frequently employed techniques for financial statement analysis.

These methods of analysis essentially consider the past financial results of the organization and the analysis of these statements is treated like a post-mortem whereas financial analytics is a forward-looking approach wherein the datasets and patterns of the data are studied to derive or predict the future of the company. Analytics delves into the future of the organization and uses the modeling approach in its algorithms. The differences between the both is represented below in the table and graph.

RATIO ANALYSIS					
Growth Ratios	2016	2015	Activity Ratios	2016	2015
Sales Growth	25.0%	5.8%	Receivable Turnover	2.2	2.1
Income Growth	24.6%	-1.1%	Inventory Turnover	1.4	1.9
Asset Growth	58.0%	27.1%	Fixed Asset Turnover	0.6	0.7
Profitability Ratios	2016	2015	Liquidity Ratios	2016	2015
Profit Margin	46.6%	46.8%	Current Ratio	3.44	3.26
Return on Assets	33.1%	38.3%	Quick Ratio	2.31	2.47
Return on Equity	62.1%	81.8%	Solvency Ratios	2016	2015
Dividend Payout Ratio	5.3%	6.7%	Debt to Total Assets	0.28	0.42
Price Earnings Ratio	31.4	27.4			

Example of Financial Analysis Figure 1

Typically for example, the growth ratios like sales growth, income growth or asset growth are analyzed for the last few years.

Similarly, in the case of activity ratios like the receivable's turnover, inventory turnover, fixed assets turnover etc. the efficiency of the company in managing the assets can be revealed.

On the other hand, by analyzing the above ratios for the last few years, one can predict how the future would look like. (See Figure 1)

Take for example, the case of solar energy production (in GWh), by analyzing the data on a daily basis or a weekly basis one can predict the future production. (See Figure 2)

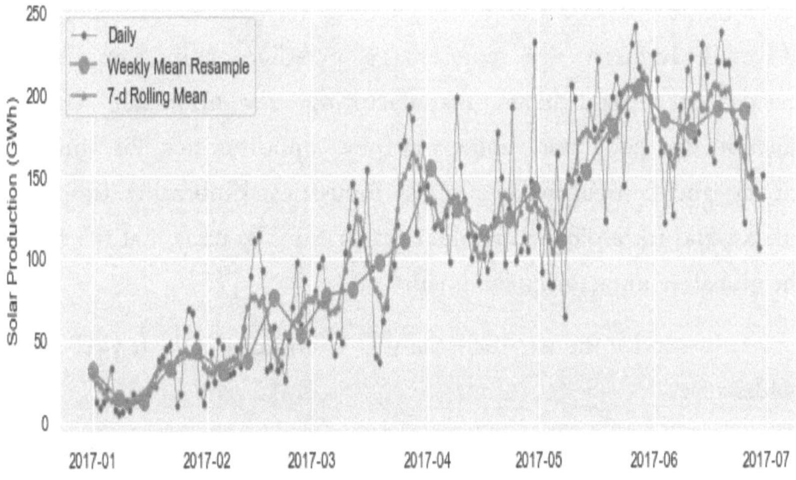

Example of Financial Analytics (Figure 2)

3.6 Implication of Industry 4.0 in Financial Analytics:

Industry 4.0 uses cutting-edge technologies to construct highly connected, intelligent, and efficient production systems, building on the automation, mass manufacturing, and mechanization that defined earlier industrial revolutions. Fundamentally, Industry 4.0 seeks to integrate digital technology throughout the whole value chain to increase productivity, flexibility, and customization while decreasing costs and time- to-market.

Among the major technologies advancing Industry 4.0 are:

1. The Internet of Things (IOT)

2. Analytics and Big Data

3. Machine learning and artificial intelligence (ML and AI).

4. Robotics and Automation

5. Additive Manufacturing (3D Printing)

6. Cyber-Physical Systems (CPS)

7. Augmented Reality (AR) and

8. Virtual Reality (VR)

Overall, Industry 4.0 represents a paradigm shift towards smart, connected, and data-driven manufacturing, revolutionizing traditional production methods and unlocking new opportunities for innovation, efficiency, and competitiveness across industries. Embracing Industry 4.0 principles and technologies enables organisations to remain at the forefront of the global manufacturing landscape.

Even in-service industry especially E-Commerce industry, AI and ML are widely used.

They are used especially in the areas of credit rating, treasury management, risk analysis, investment strategies etc.in the field of finance

Big data, financial analytics, AI, ML etc are predominantly used by the ecommerce industry like Amazon, Flipkart, etc to understand the consumer behaviour patterns like products frequently bought, the average value of the basket of items bought by the customers, location of the customer etc.

3.7 Overview of financial analytics and its importance in B2C businesses

In a business-to-consumer (B2C) context, financial data analytics is particularly crucial for understanding consumer behaviour, optimizing marketing strategies, improving customer experience, and ultimately driving profitability. Here's an overview of its importance in B2C businesses:

1. **Consumer Insights**: Financial data analytics helps B2C businesses gain deeper insights into consumer behaviour by analysing transactional data, demographic information, and purchasing patterns.

2. **Marketing Optimization**: By analysing financial data related to marketing efforts, such as advertising spend, customer acquisition costs, and campaign performance metrics, debtor turnover ratio, inventory turnover ratio, sales growth to market growth ratios, B2C businesses can optimize their marketing strategies for maximum effectiveness. Financial analytics allows businesses to identify which marketing channels, messages, and campaigns yield the highest return on investment (ROI).

3. **Revenue Maximization**: Financial data analytics enables B2C businesses to identify opportunities for revenue maximization and pricing optimization. By analysing pricing data, sales volumes, customer segmentation, branding data of campaign performance, businesses can define the desired pricing strategy for their products or services, maximizing revenue while remaining competitive in the market.

4. **Customer Retention and Loyalty:** B2C companies can create plans to improve customer loyalty and retention by compiling financial data on client turnover, retention rates, and lifetime value. In order to improve customer lifetime value and lower churn rates, financial

analytics assists firms in identifying at-risk customers, predicting attrition, and implementing targeted retention activities.

5. **Risk Management:** For B2C companies, financial data analytics is essential to manage risk as it helps them recognize and reduce possible risks associated with fraud, credit default, and regulatory compliance. Businesses can act to stop fraud and reduce financial losses by evaluating transactional data and looking for unusual patterns.

6. **Operational Efficiency:** By pointing up opportunities for resource conservation, process optimization, and cost reduction, financial data analytics may help B2C companies operate more efficiently.

3.8 Introduction to key concepts, tools, and techniques used in financial data analysis

A foundational grasp of the ideas and procedures necessary for efficiently analyzing financial data is provided via an introduction to the major concepts, instruments, and techniques utilized in financial data analysis.

1. **Essential Concepts:**

   - Financial Data: Recognising the many forms of financial data, such as cash flow statements, income statements, balance sheets, and financial ratios.

   - Time Value of Money: Developing the notion that variables like interest and inflation cause money to have varying values over time.

   - Risk and Return: Examining how risk and return in financial investments relate to one another and how that relationship affects investment choices.

   - Financial Ratios: Gain knowledge of the important financial ratios, such as solvency, liquidity, and profitability ratios, that are used to evaluate the performance and financial health of businesses.

The above concepts are also explained in detail in chapter 1.

2. **Tools:**

- Spreadsheet Software: For organising, analysing, and visualising financial data, spreadsheet programs like Microsoft Excel or Google Sheets are used.

  Using financial data in a spreadsheet is a common practice for tracking, analysing, and managing finances. The following are the ways to organise and use financial data effectively on spreadsheets.

Basic Financial Data Organization

- **Rows for Records:** Each row typically represents an individual financial transaction or record.

- **Columns for Categories:** Columns can be used for date, description, category, amount, and any other relevant fields like payment method, account, etc.

- **Categorization:** Group similar types of financial transactions (e.g., income, expenses, assets, liabilities) using a clear category or label.

3. **Financial Calculations**

- **Summation:**

  Use =SUM(range)to add up total values for a range of cells, such as calculating total expenses or revenue.

- **Averages:**

  Use =AVERAGE (range) to find the average of a range of values, useful for calculating average expenses or returns.

- **Percentage Calculations:**

  Use =value/total to find the percentage share of a value compared to a total (e.g., expense category as a percentage of total income).

- **Running Totals:**

  Use =SUM (B2: B2) to create a running total, where the range dynamically extends with each row.

4. **Income & Expense Tracking**

   - Track monthly income and expenses by creating columns for each month and summing or averaging the totals for budgeting.

   - Use a category breakdown to see how much you're spending in each area (e.g., housing, utilities, groceries, transportation).

5. **Cash Flow Statements**

   - Set up columns for inflows (income) and outflows (expenses), with a net cash flow column that calculates the difference between the two.

   - Use filters or pivot tables to quickly see the breakdown by category or time period.

6. **Budgeting**

   - Compare **actual** financial data to **budgeted** amounts by placing them side by side.

   - Use conditional formatting to highlight areas where actual spending exceeds the budget.

7. **Loan Calculations**

   - Use financial functions like =PMT (rate, periods, loan amount) to calculate loan repayments or =FV (rate, periods, payment) to calculate future value.

8. **Salary and Bonus Calculations**

   - Track salary data with allowances and bonuses in separate columns.

   - Use formulas to compute total income by adding salary, allowance, and bonus.

- For taxes or deductions, subtract the relevant amounts using =salary - tax - deductions.

9. **Financial Ratios**

   - Use formulas to calculate financial ratios like profit margin (=net profit/revenue), return on investment (ROI), or debt-to-income ratio.

10. **Visualization**

   - Create charts (bar, pie, line charts) to visually represent financial data like income trends, expense categories, or cash flow patterns.

11. **Data Validation and Protection**

   - Use **data validation** to restrict input to specific values or ranges (e.g., prevent negative numbers in an income column).

   - Apply **password protection** to sensitive financial spreadsheets to limit access.

Example1:

The following table depicts the orders received by the customers, revenue and profit earned on the order, profit margin and revenue growth in percentage. This data helps the management in deciding the quantum of profit made on each order and also supports the organisation in understanding the importance to be given to the customer as per the requirement. The data can be utilised to predict the behaviour of the customer. For the large amount of financial data, the sorting function of excel can guide the organisation to arrive at conclusions of priority customers.

Q1 Orders

Customer Number	Customer Name	Order Number	Revenue	Profit	Profit margin	Revenue Growth
11803	Vijay Shanthi Builders	11803-6827	675	169	25.0%	8%
14213	Thakkars Developers	14213-9073	1,109	277	25.0%	25%
15201	Kamanwala Housing Construction	15201-4134	20,237	5,059	25.0%	13%
15916	BSEL Infrastructure Realty	15916-3107	8,530	10	0.1%	7%
19800	Arihant Foundations & Housing	19800-6050	19,601	560	2.9%	7%
22787	SAAG RR Infra	22787-7678	689	172	25.0%	9%
35220	Asahi Infrastructure & Projects	35220-6145	10,021	2,505	25.0%	34%
36024	Arvind Infra	36024-2407	703	176	25.0%	9%
40002	HB Estate Developers	40002-2226	6,551	1,638	25.0%	34%
45101	Eldeco Housing	45101-1900	12,627	440	3.5%	18%
59920	Radhe Developers	59920-1055	8,886	2,221	25.0%	22%
63565	Alpine Housing Development Corporation	63565-1426	6,565	1,641	25.0%	7%
72258	Navkar Builders	72258-9485	8,404	22	0.3%	8%

Q1 Orders

Customer Number	Customer Name	Order Number	Revenue	Profit	Profit margin	Revenue Growth
76266	Maruti Infrastructure	76266-6624	12,381	66	0.5%	21%
82875	Narendra Properties	82875-3558	3,834	65	1.7%	13%
82961	Indo-Asian Projects	82961-5746	10,049	2,512	25.0%	35%
86757	Tribhuvan House	86757-1970	792	9	1.2%	14%
94398	KMF Builders and Developers	94398-8057	10,063	2,516	25.0%	42%
94398	Regaliaa Realty	94398-8057	8,745	245	2.8%	22%
94398	Mahindra Lifespace Developers	94398-8057	37,453	355	0.9%	18%

Figure 1

Note : Names are for illustrative purpose Example 2:

Name of Company EPS	
Infosys	50
TCS	35
Wipro	25
Hero Honda	20
HPCL	19
RIL	18
ABAN	16
Tata Motors	15
Patni	12
Bajaj Auto	12

RCOM	10
Company with EPS = 18	
Companies with EPS > 16	
Companies with between 20 and 30	

Figure 2

The above table summarises the EPS figures of the company on a yearly basis. In financial analytics, in the presence of large set of data of various companies, data filter option can be used to guide the companies with various EPS figures.

For example,

Company with EPS =18 can be found out through the drop-down button. It would mark towards RIL.

Companies with EPS>16

- Statistical Software: For more complex data analysis and modelling, specialised financial analysis software or statistical software packages like R or Python (with libraries like Pandas and NumPy) are used.

- Data Visualisation Tools: To build aesthetically pleasing and educational charts, graphs, and dashboards, data visualisation tools such as Tableau, Power BI, or matplotlib/seaborn in Python are used.

12. **Methods:**

- Descriptive Statistics: To summarise and characterise financial data, descriptive statistics like mean, median, mode, standard deviation, and variance are used.

- Inferential Statistics: Based on sample data, inferential statistics techniques such as regression analysis, correlation analysis, and hypothesis testing are used to draw conclusions and make predictions.

- Time-Series Analysis: Using methods including trend analysis, moving averages, and decomposition, analyse time-series data to find patterns, trends, and seasonality.

- Financial Modelling: Using methods like discounted cash flow (DCF) analysis and scenario analysis, financial models are built to simulate and forecast financial situations, assess investment opportunities, and carry out sensitivity analysis.

13. **Legal and Ethical Aspects:**

- Data Security and Privacy: Realising the value of safeguarding private financial information and making sure that data privacy laws—like the The California Consumer Privacy Act (CCPA) and General Data Protection Regulation (GDPR)—are followed.

- Confidentiality: Preserving integrity and secrecy when managing financial data, particularly when working with proprietary or private data.

- Ethical Use of Data: Preserving impartiality and averting conflicts of interest while gathering, analysing, and interpreting financial data in accordance with moral standards.

3.9 Application of Data Analytics and Financial Analytics

Financial analytics finds numerous applications across various sectors and functions within the finance industry. Here are some common applications:

1. **Investment Decision Making:**

   To analyse investment opportunities, gauge risk, and maximise portfolio allocations, investors, portfolio managers, and financial institutions heavily rely on financial analytics. To find reasonable assets, forecast market trends, and improve investment strategies, analysts use methods including technical, fundamental, and quantitative research.

2. **Risk Management:**

   Market risk, credit risk, operational risk, and liquidity risk are just a few of the hazards that financial analytics is essential in identifying and controlling. Organisations can evaluate and reduce possible risks with the aid of risk analytics tools including Monte Carlo simulations, scenario analysis, stress testing, and Value at Risk (VaR) modelling.

3. **Performance Measurement:**

   Investment portfolios, financial products, and business units are all evaluated for performance using financial analytics. To evaluate the success of investment strategies and pinpoint areas for development, performance indicators including return on investment (ROI), Sharpe ratio, alpha, and beta are computed.

4. **Financial Planning and Forecasting:**

   With the use of financial analytics, businesses may create precise cash flow projections, budgets, and financial forecasts. Through the examination of past data and the identification of significant factors influencing financial performance, entities can arrive at well-informed decisions concerning the distribution of resources, capital needs, and targeted investments.

5. **Credit Scoring and Risk Assessment:**

   Banks and other financial organisations use financial analytics to evaluate borrower creditworthiness and efficiently manage credit risk. Credit scoring methods that rely on borrower statistical analysis.

6. **Fraud Detection and Prevention:**

   Financial analytics is employed in the banking, insurance, and other financial transaction industries to identify and stop fraudulent activity. To find suspicious patterns, spot fraudulent transactions, and reduce the risk of fraud, advanced analytics tools including anomaly detection, pattern recognition, and machine learning algorithms are used.

7. **Customer Segmentation and Targeting:**

Banks, insurers, and suppliers of financial services divide up their clientele into groups according to their needs, preferences, and financial habits using financial analytics. By focussing marketing efforts, services, and product offerings on particular customer segments, companies can increase customer retention and satisfaction through the use of customer segmentation models.

8. **Regulatory Compliance and Reporting:**

Financial analytics helps make sure that companies are in compliance with standards for reporting and regulatory regulations. Organisations can exhibit accountability, openness, and compliance with regulations by evaluating financial data and keeping an eye on key performance metrics.

All things considered, financial analytics helps businesses make data-driven choices, allocate resources optimally, effectively manage risks, and improve overall financial performance in a fast-paced, cutthroat markets.

3.10 Application of Statistical Analysis for Finance:

Because statistical analysis offers instruments for evaluating risk, analysing financial data, and making well-informed investment decisions, it is essential to the finance industry. An outline of statistical analysis in finance is provided below:

1. **Descriptive Statistics:**

   - A dataset's properties are summarised and described using descriptive statistics.

- The mean, median, and mode are examples of central tendency measures that shed light on a dataset's typical or average value.

- Variance and standard deviation, two measures of dispersion, characterise the variability or spread of data points around the mean.

- To see and comprehend the distribution of financial data, histograms, box plots, and summary statistics are frequently utilised.

2. **Inferential Statistics:**

- Using sample data, inferential statistics assist in drawing conclusions or forecasts about the population. Using sample data, hypothesis testing entails evaluating a theory regarding a population parameter. ANOVA, chi-square, and t-tests are examples of common tests.

- Confidence intervals, which are dependent on sample data and a predetermined degree of confidence, offer a range of values that a population parameter is expected to fall inside.

- Correlation analysis quantifies the direction and intensity of a relationship between two variables, like the relationship between economic indicators or stock returns.

3. **Regression Analysis:**

This method looks at how one or more independent variables and a dependent variable are related. A straight line is used in simple linear regression to model the relationship between two variables. By analysing the relationship between a dependent variable and several independent variables at once, multiple regression expands on linear regression. In finance, regression analysis is frequently used for forecasting, risk evaluation, and portfolio optimisation.

4. **Analysis of Time Series:**

   Analysing data over time to find patterns and trends is known as time-series analysis. Trend analysis finds patterns or long-term trends in time series data, such rising or falling trends in stock prices. To comprehend seasonal trends and swings, seasonal decomposition divides a time series into its seasonal, trend, and irregular components. Exponential smoothing techniques and Autoregressive Integrated Moving Average (ARIMA) models are used for time-series forecasting in finance.

5. **Volatility Analysis:**

   Volatility quantifies how much a financial return varies or is dispersed. Variance and standard deviation measure the volatility of asset returns and convey the risk or unpredictability of a certain investment. The tendency of asset returns to show periods of high or low volatility across time is known as volatility clustering. Financial market volatility is forecasted and managed using volatility modelling approaches like GARCH (Generalised Autoregressive Conditional Heteroskedasticity) models. Investment plans, risk management, and financial markets are all greatly enhanced by statistical analysis. Finance professionals can detect trends, evaluate risk, and make well-informed decisions to meet their financial goals by using statistical approaches to analyse financial data.

Statistical analysis provides valuable insights into financial markets, risk management, and investment strategies. By applying statistical techniques to analyze financial data, finance professionals can identify trends, assess risk, and make informed decisions to achieve their financial objectives.

Essential tools for summarising and characterising a dataset's properties are descriptive statistics. An outline of frequently used descriptive statistics is provided below:

1. **Mean:**

    The mean, sometimes referred to as the average, is the central tendency of the data and a measure of the typical value. It is calculated by dividing the sum of all values in a dataset by the total number of observations.

2. **Median:**

    A dataset's median is its midway value when arranged from least to greatest. If the dataset has an odd number of observations, the median is the middle value. It is less affected by extreme values (outliers) compared to the mean and gives a measure of the central tendency that is more resilient to skewed distributions.

3. **Mode:**

    Unlike the mean and median, the mode can be used with both numerical and categorical data. It is the value that appears in a dataset the most. A dataset may have no mode if all values occur with the same frequency, or it may have one mode (unimodal), two modes (bimodal), or more than two modes (multimodal).

4. **Variance:**

    Variance quantifies how widely apart or dispersed data points are from the mean. It determines each data point's average squared departure from the mean. A low variance denotes that the data points are closely grouped around the mean, whereas a large variance denotes that the data points are widely dispersed from the mean.

5. **Standard Deviation:**

    This standardised measure of dispersion calculates the average distance between data points and the mean. It is the square root of the variance. Greater variability in the data is indicated by a higher standard deviation, and less variability is indicated by a smaller standard deviation. The central tendency, variability, and distribution of a dataset can all be better understood and interpreted by researchers, analysts, and decision-makers with the help of these descriptive statistics.

Measures of dispersion

Dispersion metrics shed light on how widely distributed, variable, or scattered data points are within a dataset. They quantify the degree to which individual data points depart from the average, which is a useful addition to measures of central tendency such as mean, median, and mode. The following are the few typical dispersion measurements:

1. **Range:**

   The difference between a dataset's maximum and minimum values is the range, which is the most basic measure of dispersion. It gives a general idea of how the data is distributed but is susceptible to outliers.

2. **Variance:**

   This quantifies the dispersion of data points around the mean and is computed by adding the squared differences between each data point and the mean. It represents the average squared deviation of each data point from the mean.

3. **Average Deviation**

   The variance's square root is the standard deviation. Considering that it is reported in the same units as the original data, it offers a measure of dispersion that is easier to understand than variance. The standard deviation, which is frequently employed in statistical analysis to evaluate variability, calculates the average distance of data points from the mean.

4. **Mean Absolute Deviation (MAD):**

   This statistic reflects how far out from the mean each data point is on average. Because MAD takes into account absolute differences rather than squared variations like variance and standard deviation do, it is less susceptible to outliers. The average of the absolute differences between each data point and the mean is used to compute MAD.

5. **Interquartile Range (IQR):**

This is a measure of dispersion that is derived from a dataset's quartiles. Compared to the range, it is less impacted by extreme numbers, or outliers, and represents the range of the middle 50% of the data. The difference between the dataset's first (Q1) and third (Q3) quartiles is used to compute the IQR.

By illuminating the variability and dispersion of data points within a dataset, these measures of dispersion provide analysts and researchers important new perspectives on the distribution and properties of the data. For evaluating variability and making defensible conclusions, several measures of dispersion may be more appropriate, depending on the nature of the data and the goals of the study.

Histograms, box plots, and summary statistics

In statistical analysis, histograms, box plots, and summary statistics are frequently used methods for visualising and summarising a dataset's distribution and properties. Below is a summary of each:

1. **Histograms:**

An analyst can identify patterns, trends, and outliers by using a histogram, which is a graphical representation of a dataset's frequency distribution made up of bars that represent the frequency or relative frequency of data points within various intervals (bins) of the data's range. Histograms are especially helpful for examining the distribution of numerical data and determining its skewness, kurtosis, and modality.

2. **Box Plots (Box-and-Whisker Plots):**

A box plot highlights the central tendency, dispersion, and variability of the data by providing a visual representation of a dataset's distribution.

- The interquartile range (IQR) of the data is represented by a box, and the median (Q2) is indicated by a line inside the box.

- The "whiskers" reach the minimum and maximum values within a specified range (often 1.5 times the IQR) from the box.

- Box plots are helpful for evaluating the symmetry and skewness of the data, finding outliers, and comparing the distributions of several datasets.

- They offer a graphic representation of important summary statistics, including the quartiles, median, and possible outliers.

Summary Statistics:

Summaries of statistics include numerical summaries of important features of a dataset, like form, dispersion, and central tendency. Typical summary data consist of:

- Mean: The dataset's average value, which shows the centre tendency.

- Median: The dataset's middle value, obtained by sorting the values from smallest to greatest; this measure of the central tendency is resistant to outliers. Measures of the distribution or dispersion of data points around the mean are provided by variance and standard deviation.

- Quartiles: Information on the distribution of the data is provided by values that split the dataset into four equal parts.

Analysers can compare datasets, evaluate the variability and distributional shape of data, and comprehend the fundamental characteristics of a dataset with the aid of summary statistics. When used in tandem, histograms, box plots, and summary statistics offer complimentary methods for illustrating and condensing a dataset's properties, giving analysts deeper understanding of its variability, central tendency, and distribution. They are necessary for testing hypotheses, doing exploratory data analysis, and reaching well-informed conclusions in a variety of disciplines, such as data science, finance, and statistics.

Inferential Statistics

ANOVA (Analysis of Variance), chi-square tests, and t-tests are popular statistical methods for data analysis and population inference. Below is a summary of each:

1. **T-tests**

    *   To compare the means of two groups and ascertain whether there is a statistically significant difference between them, t-tests are utilised.

    *   The t-statistic, which gauges the variance within each group and the difference between the means of the two groups, is computed by the t-test.

    *   T-tests come in a variety of forms, such as:

    *   To compare the means of two independent groups, use the independent samples t-test. When comparing the means of two related groups (for example, before and after measurements), the paired samples t-test is utilised.

    *   In a t-test, the null hypothesis states that there is no variation in the means of the two teams. The idea that there is a difference is the alternative hypothesis.

    *   T-tests are frequently used to compare group means and determine the significance of observed differences in a variety of professions, including psychology, medicine, and business.

2. **Analysis of Variance, or ANOVA:**

    When comparing the means of three or more groups, an ANOVA is utilized to see if there are any statistically significant differences.

The F-statistic, which contrasts the variation within and between groups, is computed by ANOVA. There are various ANOVA forms, such as:

When comparing the means of three or more independent groups, one-way ANOVA is utilized. Two-way ANOVA: Employed when evaluating the interaction between two independent variables (factors) and the dependent variable.

The ANOVA null hypothesis is similar to t-tests. or ANOVA is that the group means do not differ from one another. The idea that there is a difference is the alternative hypothesis. Regression model analysis of variance, quality assurance, and experimental research all frequently use ANOVA.

3. **Chi-square test**

To evaluate if there is a statistically significant relationship between categorical variables, chi- square tests are utilized. The chi-square statistic, which gauges the discrepancy between observed and predicted frequencies of categorical data, is computed using the chi-square test. Chi-square tests come in various varieties, such as: Chi-square test of independence: Applies to ascertain if two category variables are related. Chi-square goodness-of-fit test: This test is used to assess whether there is a significant difference between the observed and expected category frequencies. In a chi-square test, the null hypothesis states that the categorical variables are not related. The idea that there is an association is the alternative hypothesis. Chi- square tests are frequently employed in evaluating hypotheses regarding categorical data, survey research, and contingency table analysis.

In many different areas of study and application, these statistical tests offer useful instruments for data analysis, hypothesis testing, and drawing conclusions about populations. It is necessary to comprehend their applications and guiding principles in order to do thorough statistical analysis and get significant conclusions from data.

A statistical method for determining the direction and degree of a relationship between two or more variables is correlation analysis. It evaluates the degree to which variations in one variable are correlated with variations in another. An outline of correlation analysis is provided below:

4. **The coefficient of Pearson correlation:**

The linear link between two continuous variables is measured by the Pearson correlation coefficient. It falls between-1 and+1, where: Perfect positive correlation: the two variables rise in proportion to each other's increases.

Perfect negative correlation: the other variable falls proportionately as the first one rises. The variables do not exhibit a linear connection, or correlation.

5. **Spearman Rank Correlation Coefficient:**

The monotonic link between two variables is measured by the Spearman rank correlation coefficient, which also indicates its direction.

- When there is a nonlinear relationship between variables or when the variables themselves are ordinal, it is utilized.

- Like the Pearson correlation coefficient, Spearman's rho has a range of -1 to +1; however, it evaluates the monotonic relationship between variables as opposed to a linear one.

Interpretation:

- A greater association between the variables is shown by correlation coefficients closer to +1 or -1, whilst a weaker relationship is indicated by coefficients closer to 0.

- Positive correlations show that the tendency for one variable to rise also tends the other to increase, whereas negative correlations show that the tendency for one variable to decrease tends the other to increase.

- Causation is not implied by correlation. A strong correlation between two variables does not always imply that changing one would change the other.

Correlation Matrix:

The correlation coefficients between several variables are shown tabular in a correlation matrix. It gives analysts a thorough perspective of how variables relate to one another inside a dataset, making it possible to spot patterns and linkages. In order to investigate correlations between variables, pinpoint predictive elements, and assist in decision-making, correlation analysis is extensively employed in a variety of domains, including finance, economics, psychology, and social sciences. It's crucial to remember that correlation does not imply causation, and further investigation and analysis are frequently needed to determine the causal linkages between variables.

Financial forecasting, risk management, portfolio management, and asset pricing are just a few of the many uses of regression analysis in the field. Regression analysis is used in the following ways in finance:

- *CAPM or the Capital Asset Pricing Model:*

  The widely-used CAPM model in finance calculates an asset's expected return using regression analysis, considering the asset's systematic risk (beta) and risk-free rate of return.

- **Three-Factor Model Franco-French:**

  By adding more variables to explain asset returns, like size (market capitalization) and value (book-to-market ratio), the Fama-French model expands on the CAPM. Regression analysis is used to determine these components' coefficients and how they affect asset returns.

1. **Risk Management:**

To determine the relationship between the returns of various assets or portfolios, regression analysis is utilised in risk management. It assists in measuring the degree of covariance or correlation between assets, which is important for portfolio design and diversification. By simulating the link between different risk factors and asset returns, regression analysis may also be used to assess Value at Risk (VaR) and other risk indicators.

2. **Financial Forecasting:**

To predict the link between financial variables (such sales, earnings, or stock prices) and other pertinent elements, financial forecasting uses regression analysis. Based on past performance and other pertinent data, it assists analysts in forecasting future financial performance. Financial forecasting frequently makes use of time-series regression models, such as autoregressive (AR), moving average (MA), and autoregressive integrated moving average (ARIMA) models.

3. **Factor Models:**

Regression analysis is used by factor models to separate the returns of an asset or portfolio into idiosyncratic and systematic components. Based on factor exposures, these models assist investors in understanding the sources of risk and return in their portfolios and in making well- informed investment decisions.

4. **Trend Analysis:**

Time-series data can be utilised to detect and measure long-term patterns or trends using trend analysis. It aids analysts in comprehending the data's underlying trend or direction over time. Typical techniques for trend analysis consist of:

Moving averages: By averaging nearby data points over a predetermined amount of time, moving averages help to smooth out data volatility.

Linear regression: This method estimates the time series' slope (or trend) by fitting a straight line to the data.

Exponential smoothing: To estimate the trend, previous measurements are given exponentially decreasing weights.

Trend analysis extrapolates the trend into the future to assist forecast values in the future.

5. **Seasonal Disintegration:**

   A time series can be divided into its seasonal, trend, and residual components using seasonal decomposition.

   It facilitates the identification and examination of data fluctuations and seasonal patterns. Regression analysis or moving averages are commonly used to identify and eliminate the trend component in the seasonal decomposition procedure. Using techniques like seasonal indices or Fourier analysis, breaking down the detrended series into seasonal and residual components. Seasonal adjustments for forecasting can be made by analysts using seasonal decomposition to comprehend the underlying seasonality in the data.

6. **Predictive Methodologies:**

   Forecasting techniques are used to project a time series' future values based on available historical data and other pertinent details.

   Typical forecasting techniques consist of the following:

   Exponential smoothing: updates a weighted average of historical observations to predict future values, giving higher weights to more recent observations.

   Autoregressive Integrated Moving Average (ARIMA) models: These models use a linear combination of historical values that are differenced to provide stationarity to predict future values of a time series.

   Seasonal ARIMA (SARIMA) models: These models are extended to take into consideration data's seasonal patterns.

Prophecy: A forecasting tool created by Facebook that models time-series data using additive regression by breaking it down into trend, seasonality, and holiday effects.

Businesses and analysts can use forecasting methodologies to make well-informed decisions regarding budgeting, sales planning, inventory management, and resource allocation. Time-series analysis is a popular tool used to evaluate past data, identify patterns and trends, and forecast future values in a variety of disciplines, including engineering, finance, economics, and meteorology. Time-series analysis methods can provide analysts with important insights into the dynamics of time-varying facts and use their conclusions to make well-informed judgements.

3.11 Example of building a financial model to analyze B2C business performance:

Constructing a structured framework to forecast financial performance, evaluate important metrics, and make well-informed business decisions are all part of building a financial model to analyse the performance of a business-to-consumer (B2C) company. The following is a step- by-step strategy to creating a B2C company's financial model:

1. *Specify the Goal:*

   Clearly state the financial model's precise aims and objectives. For instance, are you preparing for future expansion, assessing possible investments, or assessing the performance of an already-existing B2C business?

2. *Compile Information:*

   Gather past financial information for the B2C company, such as cash flow, balance, and income statements. Compile operational information such as marketing costs, average order value, customer attrition rates, and costs associated with acquiring new customers.

Include market information, industry standards, and pertinent economic indicators in the B2C company.

3. ***Determine Important factors and Assumptions:***

   - Determine the important factors and assumptions that affect the B2C business's financial performance. These could consist of:

   - Customer acquisition rate, average transaction value, frequency of repeat purchases, and other factors are revenue generators.

   - Cost drivers include things like marketing expenditures, running costs, and customer service charges.

   - Economic factors: rates of inflation, interest rates, patterns of consumer spending, etc.

   - Based on past trends, market research, and industry expertise, make reasonable assumptions.

4. ***Create a Revenue Forecast:***

   - Create a revenue projection by estimating future sales using the assumptions and drivers that have been defined.

   - If appropriate, use other revenue streams, such as product sales, subscription income, and advertising money.

   - Consider external factors, market trends, and seasonality that could affect sales growth.

5. ***Model Costs and Expenses:***

   - Project running costs, such as those related to technology, staff, marketing, and overhead.

   - Employ past information and industry standards to forecast future expenditures and charges.

- Consider both fixed and variable costs, as well as how they could alter as thecompany grows.

6. ***Project Cash Flow:***

- During the forecast period, project cash inflows and outflows while accounting for income, expenses, investments, and financing activities.

- Examine cash flow trends to make sure the company has enough cash on hand to pay its debts and finance expansion plans.

7. ***Conduct Sensitivity Analysis:***

- This step evaluates how changes in important assumptions may affect the B2C company's financial results.

- Determine which are the main factors influencing financial performance, then assess how sensitive the model is to variations in these variables.

8. ***Verify and Examine:***

- Verify the financial model by contrasting the anticipated outcomes with past performance and industry standards.

- Check the model for correctness, consistency, and completeness; make any necessary revisions in light of comments and new information.

9. ***Produce Reports and Analysis:***

- Create dashboards, financial reports, and visualizations to convey the financial model's conclusions and insights.

- Draw attention to trends, opportunities, and areas of concern or opportunity.

- For the B2C firm, use the financial model to assist in strategic planning, decision- making, and performance tracking.

10. ***Iterate and Update:***

- As new information becomes available, market conditions shift, or business plans change, the financial model should be updated and improved continuously. Take into account stakeholder input and modify assumptions as necessary to keep the model current and applicable.

Chapter 4

Innovative Financial Analysis with Machine Learning and Artificial Intelligence

Artificial Intelligence (AI) is the intelligence of machines which simulates human intelligence designed to think and act exactly like human beings. AI systems are capable of learning, reasoning, solving problems, and understanding language. Applications range from tiny virtual assistants like Siri and Alexa through larger ones, namely autonomous vehicles, right through highly sophisticated data analysis.

Machine learning is the branch of Artificial intelligence that develops computers' ability to learn from existing data in order to make predictions or even judgements using statistical models and algorithms. Machine learning algorithms learn from examples and are capable of self-improvement. Supervised learning, unsupervised learning, and reinforcement learning are some of the major techniques applied in ML at work.

AI hosts the larger remit of creating intelligent systems, while machine learning is a particular methodology within AI that applies data-driven techniques to realize this very same intelligence. ML is a solution that adequately addresses a problem that is difficult to solve because of the complexity of the explicit rules; it can carry out tasks such as recognizing images, processing natural languages, and making recommendations. AI and ML are combined and used for the automation of complex processes, optimization of operations, and making actual innovations in technology.

Evolution and Implications of Artificial Intelligence and Machine Learning in Finance Artificial Intelligence (AI) and Machine Learning

(ML) in financial services have been transforming, changing the operations and decision-making landscape of financial institutions. AI and ML started off with predictive models and automated algorithms handling some simple tasks. Recent large improvements in algorithms, computational power, and data availability enable improvements in sophistication. AI chatbots and virtual assistants are the latest transformation in customer services, being efficient and effective with every customer that gets personalized help. AI and ML have improved prediction accuracy, optimized decision-making, and increased operational efficiency within finance.

Current Trends and Adoption rates in financial institutions

Technology, either on the edges of AI or ML, has done much to advance the financial services segment at an extremely quick pace. One of the greatest trends in this field is rise in the usage of data analytics. Recently, financial institutions have been using huge chunks of data for actionable insight to make better decisions. AI- and ML-driven predictive analytics is applied in the evaluation of risks in investments and to predict market trends with higher degrees of accuracy. Data-enabled capabilities of this sort allow firms to make quicker course corrections to capture better market opportunities.

Another one of the major trends is the automation of a number of processes within the financial industry. At the same time, AI-powered technologies in transaction processing, compliance checks, and reporting will become increasingly capable of automating the end-to-end processes, thereby reducing the operational cost and leading to lower human-made errors in efficiency and reliability when performing routine tasks. Moreover, the growing use of robo- advisors marks a significant shift in the delivery of investment services. These AI-powered platforms provide personalized investment advice and portfolio management at a lower cost than human financial advisors can, so more customers can access such services. The adoption of AI and ML for fraud detection and risk management is also on the rise. Financial institutions are adopting advanced algorithms that automatically analyze transactional data in less than a second and enable businesses to grasp the suspicious activity in the bud, hence reducing losses from fraud and improving security. The financial sector itself has seen an increased adaption with AI, as by 2023, nearly 70% of the firms in the sector reported having integrated AI into at least one of their operational functions, according to a McKinsey report 2023. The growing investment in AI technologies comes as another reinforcement of the domain's disposition toward innovation for better efficiency and customer service. Further, the traditional financial institutions are increasingly partnering with fintech companies to accelerate the adoption of AI-powered solutions. The collaboration enables the bank to adopt faster innovation for better service and, most importantly, in areas related to payment processing, loaning, and customer collaboration. Furthermore, the financial landscape is continuously changing, and greater attention is given to ethical AI practice.

Building customer trust is very important for ensuring fairness, transparency, and accountability of AI algorithms, while generally, finance has shown a rapid movement towards becoming more technology and customer-oriented.

AI and machine learning are remodelling the finance industry, from a simple application to enhancing efficiency, improving customer experience, and informing better decision-making. The use cases:

Fraud Detection and Prevention: AI and ML algorithms analyze the pattern of transactions in real time to identify suspicious activities and flag probable frauds. By learning from historical data, the systems adapt and improve their detection capabilities by reducing false positives with enhanced security.

Credit Scoring and Risk Assessment: Conventional credit-scoring methodology has been extended to include AI and ML model analysis of a far greater sphere of influence, including social media activity and transaction history. This can provide a much more accurate determination of creditworthiness on which lenders can make much better-informed decisions regarding lending.

Algorithmic Trading: AI-powered algorithms trading, when analyzing market trends along with historical data and news events, prompt them to make trades at the most opportune time. These are capable of reacting to changing market conditions in milliseconds and hence result in more potent strategies in trading and better returns on investments.

Personalized Banking and Financial Services: AI chatbots and virtual assistants enhance customer services through recommendation and personalized support. The system will be able to study customers' behaviour and their preferences with a view to making recommendations on offers regarding financial products and services, which would further help improve customer engagement and satisfaction. For instance, robo-advisory services involve intelligent algorithms that consider investment guidance automatically and according to a personal risk profile and set financial goals. This makes investment management more democratic by allowing a wider audience access to professional investment strategy, though at lesser cost.

Regulatory Compliance: Processes on checks-like anti-money laundering and undertakings- like know-your-customer can be accomplished with the automation help of AI and ML. Such systems can analyze vast amounts of data for assurance of compliance and identify potential regulatory issues.

AI-powered tools analyze big datasets and make predictions about market trends. Integrating various data sources, such as social media sentiment together with economic indicators, into their systems truly makes them insightful for investment strategies and risk management.

Insurance Underwriting and Claims Processing: AI is being applied in the insurance industry to support underwriting in the analysis of data related to the customer and modification of risk by predictions. ML algorithms also automate claim processing assessments and further detect fraudulent claims with efficacy.

Customer Segmentation and Targeting: AI and ML are used in customer segmentation in financial institutions to ensure the identification of the customer group. Targeting makes it possible for them to develop focused marketing strategies with respect to different groups of customers by mining the data for the taking up of targeted campaigns.

Predictive maintenance for financial systems: AI can be applied to monitor the operating performance of a financial system with an exclusive aim of detecting abnormalities that would hint at the threat of failure. In terms of maintenance, it makes sure a system is reliable and minimizes any chances of downtimes for the best practice in general operational efficiency.

In a nutshell, the use cases of AI and ML in finance are much diversified and keep developing with technology development. Driven by such advanced technologies, financial institutions can raise their efficiency in operations, manage risks more effectively, and provide more personalized services to customers.

4.6 Data Sources and Processing

In finance, data sources and processing are integral to informed decision-making, risk assessment, and strategic planning. Financial data originates from various sources, including stock exchanges, central banks, regulatory filings, financial news platforms, and market data providers like Bloomberg and Reuters. These sources offer diverse datasets on stock prices, corporate financials, economic indicators, and industry trends. Additionally, alternative data sources—such as credit card transactions, social media sentiment, satellite imagery, and web traffic—provide unique insights into market behaviour and consumer trends, enhancing traditional financial models. Data processing in finance involves cleaning, aggregating, and structuring this data to make it actionable. Advanced processing techniques leverage data engineering and tools such as SQL, Python, and R for extracting and transforming large datasets, while big data technologies, such as Hadoop and Spark, enable processing at scale. Machine learning models and AI algorithms are also applied to identify patterns, forecast trends, and automate decision-making processes. Together, these sources and processing methods form a robust framework, supporting financial analytics, algorithmic trading and credit scoring.

Data Collection and Integration

In finance, data collection and integration are crucial for accurate risk assessment, portfolio management, compliance, and customer insights. Financial data is collected from numerous sources, including stock exchanges, regulatory filings, trading platforms, economic reports, and alternative data providers. These datasets are diverse and may include structured data, such as transaction records and financial statements, as well as unstructured data, like news articles, social media sentiment, and customer feedback. Integrating this data involves consolidating information from these varied sources into centralized databases or data lakes, often using Extract, Transform, Load (ETL) pipelines. This integration is essential for ensuring data accuracy and consistency across systems, especially for applications like real-time trading, where decisions rely on rapid data availability. Financial institutions also use APIs to pull in real-time data from third-party providers, maintaining continuous data flow for activities like algorithmic trading, fraud detection, and credit risk assessment. This integrated data environment supports advanced analytics, machine learning models, and AI tools that drive predictive insights, automate compliance monitoring, and enhance customer service. By establishing robust data collection and integration practices, financial firms can leverage a comprehensive view of financial information, fostering timely and data-driven decision- making.

Data Cleaning and Pre-processing

Data cleaning and pre-processing in finance are essential for ensuring that financial analyses, models, and algorithms operate on accurate and consistent data. Given the high volume and variety of financial data from stock exchanges, economic indicators, transactional data, and alternative sources, data often contains errors, missing values, duplicates, and inconsistencies that can compromise decision-making. Cleaning this data involves several steps, such as handling missing values by either imputing them or removing incomplete records, detecting and removing duplicates, and standardizing formats across different datasets (e.g., date and currency formats). Financial data also frequently requires the detection and correction of outliers, especially when dealing with time series data in stock prices, trading volumes, or market indices, where sudden spikes or drops can distort analysis.

Pre-processing further prepares the data for analysis, transforming it into formats suitable for machine learning and statistical models. This often involves normalization or scaling, particularly for variables with differing ranges, such as prices and trading volumes, to prevent any single feature from unduly influencing the model. Additionally, feature engineering may be employed to create new variables, such as calculating moving averages or volatility metrics, which add predictive power to financial models. Text data, like news and social media sentiment, often undergoes natural language processing (NLP) techniques to extract relevant insights. Together, data cleaning and pre-processing establish a reliable data foundation, enabling accurate financial forecasting, risk modelling, algorithmic trading, and customer analytics.

Machine Learning Techniques in Finance

Machine Learning (ML) techniques have significantly risen to play an essential role in the finance sector, from streamlining better decision-making processes to redefining operations and customer experiences.

Some of the key ML techniques in finance along with their applications are listed below:

Supervised Learning

It involves the training of models over labelled datasets; hence, they are aware of the outputs along with respective inputs. The key techniques are as below:

Regression Analysis: It helps to predict continuous outcomes, such as stock prices or loan default probabilities. Various techniques can be performed, which include linear regression, polynomial regression, and support vector regression (SVR).

Classification Algorithms: It helps in classifying data into discrete classes. Some usual techniques applied to this purpose are logistic regression, decision trees, random forests, and support vector machines (SVM). These are also used in credit scoring, fraud detection, and customer segmentation

Unsupervised Learning

Unsupervised learning techniques analyses unlabeled data to determine if there are any patterns in alternatives or groupings. Key techniques include

Clustering: This is based on the grouping of similar data points. The common algorithms used are; K-means, hierarchical clustering, and DBSCAN, which are practical in customer segmentation, market trends, and portfolio diversification.

Dimensionality Reduction:

Principal Component Analysis (PCA) and t-Distributed Stochastic Neighbour Embedding (t- SNE) techniques reduce the number of features while keeping important information. This helps in an easy visualization of complex financial data and leading to better modelling and model performance.

Ensemble Learning

Boosting: Algorithms namely AdaBoost and Gradient Boosting train models sequentially, where every model focuses on improving the mistakes of the previous one. These algorithms have been proven effective in classification and regression problems and are widely used in credit risk evaluation studies.

Reinforcement Learning

Reinforcement learning is, at its core, a type of training models through trial and error to maximize rewards. Application in Finance include

Algorithmic Trading Models learn trading decisions based on historical data and optimize buy/sell strategies through continuous learning and adjustment.

Reinforcement learning-based algorithms allow the model to dynamically adjust asset allocations in response to changing market conditions to maximize returns while minimizing risks.

Machine Learning Approaches

Techniques, such as isolation forests and one-class SVM, become very powerful tools for identifying fraudulent activities by learning the pattern of normal behaviour.

Finance is an industry in which machine learning is transforming the sector by making available tools related to analysis, prediction, and decision-making. From supervised and unsupervised learning to deep and reinforcement learning, these techniques enable financial institutions to harness the power of data, enable operational efficiency, manage risks, and improve customer experiences. Integration of machine learning enables innovation as well as competition in the sector.

AI in Financial Forecasting and Predictions

Artificial Intelligence (AI) has changed the financial forecasting and predictions paradigm, providing more accurate and faster insights in virtually all domains. This has resulted in a shift towards the use of technology in market predictions, macroeconomic modelling, and sentiment analysis. These could be incorporated in the following manner:

Market Predictions

The following are some of the critical predictions that are enabled by AI in the different markets:

Stock Prices: Through the study of historical stock price data and other relevant features, such as trading volume and volatility, among others, machine learning algorithms, including neural networks and support vector machines, are used to forecast future price movements.

These models can change their adaptiveness to the changing market state and increase their predictive powers.

Commodity Prices: AI is used in the prediction of commodity prices, such as oil, gold, and agricultural products. The process can easily network with various data sources representing historical prices, measures of supply and demand, and geopolitical events that allow the predictive models for actionable insights on the part of traders and investors.

Economic Indicators: With the use of AI, it will be possible to forecast major economic indicators, such as interest rates and consumer spending. AI models provide valuable insights through the analysis of complicated datasets and pattern detection, thereby facilitating financial institutions and policymakers to anticipate changes in the economic environment.

Macroeconomic Modelling

AI significantly enhances the accuracy of macroeconomic models so that better forecasts of broader economic conditions can be made.

GDP Growth Rate: AI algorithms analyse various indicators from consumer behaviour to investments by businesses and export-import data for predictions of the GDP growth rate. With the machine learning technique, an economist will have more advanced models that let him study nonlinear relationships and complex interactions among variables

Inflation: Expectations of rates of inflation are very much in framing the monetary policy and investment policy. AI models analyse the price indices, wage growth and consumer demand to generate forecasts that assist central banks and financial analysts in making informed decision making. They generate the forecasts of each country that help the central banks and financial analysts make informed decisions on the interest rates and fiscal policies.

Unemployment Rates: AI methods may be applied to predict unemployment rates by synthesizing labour market and dynamic job availability data with the hiring rate and the economic activity. Such a prediction can be used to inform policy for appropriate intervention in the labour market and the development of economic recovery strategies.

Sentiment Analysis

Sentiment analysis can be enhanced with next-generation Natural Language Processing to determine the sentiment level being felt toward the market. It can give valuable information on what the market feels towards certain ideas, and at the same time, lead to behaviour changes in investors and market trends.

News Analysis: AI models can analyse news articles and financial reports to extract the sentiment and key themes that might move markets. By measurably qualitating sentiments, such models are providing quantified information about the market conditions and potential changes in prices to the vast minority of participants. Social Media Listening: Social media platforms are rich grounds for real-time sentiment data. AI can process large chunks of social media posts to gauge the sentiment of the public regarding specific stocks, commodities, or market trends. This aids investors in comprehending market psychology for timely investment decisions

AI is at the forefront of revolutionizing financial forecasting and prediction across different areas, which include market predictions, macroeconomic modelling, and sentiment analysis. Using advanced algorithms and extensive datasets, AI helps make well-informed decisions, manage risk effectively, and optimize investment strategies in financial institutions. The continuous improvement in AI technologies is going to lead to much deeper integration into financial forecasting, creating enhanced accuracies and innovations in the finance sector.

Future of AI & ML

The future of Artificial Intelligence (AI) and Machine Learning (ML) in the finance sector is looking up to transformative advancements driven by emerging technologies, evolving workforce dynamics, and changing industry landscapes.

Emerging Trends

Quantum Computing: Quantum computing is the latest remarkable breakthrough in computer processing power. It allows processing complex calculations at previously unknown speeds. In the financial world, this technology will enable better assessment of risk, optimal portfolios, and algo trading strategy improvements. Using quantum algorithms, there can be achieved even higher performance and the solving of problems that remain out of reach for already existing classical computers.

Explainable AI (XAI): This is one of the expectations brought by the growth in complexity of AI models: a growing interest in explain ability and transparency. XAI provides insight into how AI models make decisions, thus ensuring stakeholders understand the rationale behind predictions. This will be key in terms of regulatory compliance for consumer trust in domains like credit scoring and loan approvals for consumers.

AI-Driven Personalization: The financial services of the future will be more personalized, and AI will support customer segmentation, targeting, and behaviour-based offerings. Predictive analytics shall enable a new level of customer experience through being able to proactively recommend options for further engagement, optimized pricing strategies, and proactive financial advice.

Prediction on AI's Impact on the Finance Industry

Enhanced Decision-Making: AI will further improve decision-making in finance by driving real-time insights and predictive analytics. With time, the dependence of financial institutions on AI will accordingly increase in terms of risk assessment, optimization of trading strategies, and recommendations on investment opportunities to be acted on in more informed and timely ways.

Enhanced Efficiency and Lowered Costs: The automation of repetitive tasks and processes, caused by AI, will in turn enhance efficiency and lower operational costs. Institutions will have streamlined operations to channel resources better and, therefore, improved productivity.

Improved Risk Management: AI will definitely improve the current practice of risk management due to the identification of risks in real time with precise risk assessment and market condition monitoring. Institutions will use advanced algorithms for the identification of emerging risks and taking proactive measures to counter them.

Increased Regulatory Compliance: AI will enable compliance in the ever-evolving regulatory environment through automation of information reporting and increasing fraud detection. Organizations will have more effective capability to detect any suspicious activity and remain within the regulatory environment, avoiding other potential penalties leading to reputational damage.

Financial Inclusion: AI has the potential to enhance financial inclusion, thereby boosting literacy on the use of formal financial services by the world's most marginalized populations. Advanced models of credit scoring, strengthened by AI, analyze non-conventional data sources to provide access to credit where traditional sources could not.

The future of AI and ML in finance points to promising developments and disruptive changes. The rise of emerging trends, like quantum computing and explainable AI, proclaims an overdue step change in the industry towards more effective decision-making, efficiencies, and better risk management. As workers evolve, other workers like financial professionals will be adapted, upskilled, and will ultimately be working in collaboration with AI. Finally, the influence of AI will shape a more inclusive, more efficient, and more innovative financial industry, leading the way into the future of a new age in financial services.

Tools and Technologies of AI and ML in Finance

Applications of Artificial Intelligence and Machine Learning based in Finance rely on a plethora of Tools and Technologies that ease their Development, Deployment, and Integration with other systems.

Few Popular AI and ML Tools and Platforms

TensorFlow is an open-source machine learning frame designed by Google for building and training models. Its versatility holds the capacity to build complex neural network structures for a wide number of applications, such as predictive analytics, risk, and algorithmic trading systems. On-the-fly prototyping can be conducted via high-level APIs, while low-level APIs can be used for fine-tuning.

PyTorch, developed by the Facebook AI Research lab, is gaining popularity with its ease of use and dynamic computation graph. This makes it particularly suited to research and experimentation, mostly in the development of deep learning models. It is the first choice for data scientists and researchers who work with finance.

Keras: Keras is a high-level neural network API, originally developed on top of TensorFlow. It is designed to take away the pain of building and training deep learning-based models, so even novices in the arena of AI and ML are not lagging behind. With high-level, user-friendly APIs, Keras speeds any kind of building, training, and testing of the model.

Scikit-Learn is a widely used traditional machine learning library in Python. It performs several tools for data preprocessing, feature selections, and model evaluation—thus a real boon to a financial analyst who wants to practice predictive modeling but doesn't want to go in that depth of learning.

H2O.ai: H2O is an open-source AI platform that offers a variety of machine learning algorithms and data analysis. It is more established with AutoML features, which are actually automated machine model training with hyperparameter tuning, that allow financial professionals to focus on advanced insights.

Integration with Blockchain among other Emerging Technologies

The integration of the AI capability into Blockchain and a host of other emerging technologies is now transforming the equipped financial landscape.

AI algorithms can study blockchain data to attempt to identify patterns, prevent fraud, and predict market trends. Furthermore, AI-powered smart contracts will automatically take optimized actions based on specified conditions.

Internet of Things: The AI convergence with IoT allows financial institutions to perform analytics on real-time data coming from these connected devices, which gives a much better opportunity for risk assessment and personalized customer experience. For example, the use of IoT sensors in the supply chain can provide signals of a potential asset valuation and the insurance underwriting process.

Robotic Process Automation: This technology can be taken one step forward through AI, automating routine activities within finance, such as data entry, report generation, and compliance checking. The integration of AI within this RPA process makes the automation intelligent, minimizing human errors and increasing operational efficiency.

Augmented Reality (AR) and Virtual Reality (VR) are two other developing technologies that, at an early stage, might complement customer engagement and training experiences at the confluence of AI application within finance. For example, VR may be incorporated to avail an immersive training environment for financial professionals with AR streaming out real-time data visualization in an investment analysis process.

A wide range of tools and technologies help support AI and ML in finance, and these are continuously evolving. By using TensorFlow, PyTorch, and Keras platforms, it helps to gradually increase the model's complexity within financial institutions. The scalability and collaboration are without bounds with the help of cloud computing. Connected integration with AI and now-evolving technologies, such as Blockchain, will offer more security, efficiency, and transparency in conducting financial operations.

Ethics, Governance and Responsible AI in Finance

Application of latest technologies like Artificial Intelligence and Machine Learning within financial services makes the considerations about ethics, transparency and accountability even more serious. Responsible AI practice ensures that these technologies are used in ways that will treat both fairness and integrity of the consumers. The vital features that can attain ethical frameworks and governance in AI for finance:

Designing Ethical Frameworks

In creating a framework of ethical AI, principles and guidelines that serve the creation and deployment of AI systems in finance, particularly with respect to what is created, developers should note down few points.

Fairness: In any model, fairness is crucial to withhold, to avoid discrimination and bias in the process of algorithmic decision-making. It would thus mean that the models are trained on diversified datasets that more or less give a true snapshot of the varied demography

Transparency: AI systems should be transparent in their operations so that stakeholders can understand the process by which any decision is reached. This is realized through accurate documentation of data sources, description of algorithms, and the process used to create the model, thus creating trust amongst consumers and regulators.

A framework for ethical principles should define the accountability for the actions of AI applications namely, who is responsible for the result of applying the AI system and or enforcing grievance processes in case any event or error occurs.

Privacy and Security: The privacy and security of consumer data form the backbone of AI ethical frameworks. Institutions should ensure that their AI systems do not provide any loopholes in data protection legislation and there are adequate data security measures to protect sensitive financial information.

Transparency and Accountability in AI-Driven Financial Services:

Transparency and Accountability become very critical to maintain consumer trust and meet the guidelines of regulations in financial services adopted with AI. Some major avenues are:

Transparent AI: Through the adoption of techniques under the banner of XAI, clear explanations can be given for decisions driven by AI, especially at financial institutions in aspects such as credit scoring and loan approvals. Such transparency would give consumers an understanding of how the data pertaining to them is utilized and for what purposes certain decisions were taken.

Regular Audits: Periodic auditing of AI systems can be done to help identify biases, inaccuracies, and compliance issues. Financial institutions need to organize review processes of the AI model's performance concerning benchmark systems on matched data to ensure compliance with ethical standards and regulatory requirements.

Feedback Mechanism: Create channels of providing feedback from consumers to understand how AI systems are working on the ground. Such feedback can be very useful to see if there are any problems and to predict the necessary changes for increased accountability.

The linking of Artificial Intelligence (AI) into the financial sector is reshaping the entire industry. On the one hand, it improves forecasting and predictions but, on the other, optimizes risk management and operational efficiency issues.

AI and ML inclusions in financial services continue to mature with such fast pace, encouraging innovation and altering landscapes. As these technologies mature, the promise they hold in advancing financial services further while driving better decisions on more complex issues becomes more evident. In addition to this, the balance should always be sustained between the considerations of ethics and compliance with regulatory demands in a way that assures sustainable advancement.

AI and ML in finance, therefore, bring with them more opportunities and challenges for the future. It is in such dynamically changing landscapes that financial institutions operate using AI wisely to ensure that technology fulfils its strategic goals as well as the greater interests of the consumers and stakeholders. Therefore, the finance industry, by adopting these technologies responsibly, unlocks the fullest potential to bring about positive change and deliver value within the ever-changing financial ecosystem.

Chapter 5

Data Visualization

5.1 Introduction

Data visualization encompasses the pictorial representation of data through charts, graphs, and maps. It helps in viewing patterns and trends in and outliers of data, thereby bringing into better accessibility and comprehension complexity in information. By converting raw data into visual elements, data visualization helps in finding the relationship among the variables, tracking the changes over time, and comparing different sets of data. It is a expansive tool common in business, healthcare, and finance that facilitates informed decision-making, insight communication, and the art of storytelling using data.

Visualization capabilities are the backbone in today's data-driven world. A good visualization expresses more in a second than what volumes of pages could do that is, convey key messages across immediately and have stakeholders reach desired insights at one glance. Data visualization plays a very important role in translating abstract data into actionable intelligence, be it through dashboards, reports, or presentations.

5.2 Process Flow of Data Visualization

Data visualization is one of the major portions of the lifecycle that goes through multiple stages of data collection, storage, transformation, mining, and presentation. How the process actually works has been explained below with the different stages of data visualization:

Data Collection: Data is collected from different places including transactional databases, social media, operational systems, web logs, etc. This data could be structured, semi-structured, or unstructured.

Data Warehousing: In the data warehouse, the gathered data is summarized and hence it acts as a central repository. In that warehouse, data are arranged in such a way so that they are easily retrieved and analyzed. The main processes include **ETL (Extract, Transform, Load),** wherein data are cleaned, changed, and loaded into the warehouse.

Data Preprocessing: Data is pre-processed before the mining process. This will include **cleaning, normalization, and transformation** in line with the requirements needed to analyze the data. In general, missing values are always handled as well as scaling or formatting data according to other analytical tools.

Data Mining: Here, algorithms are applied to find patterns and associations in the data. That includes clustering, classification, and rules of association. It is a discovery of new trends unseen before and can thereafter be visualized.

Data Visualization: Data after mining is converted into visuals, including charts, graphs, dashboards, or even heatmaps. These visualization tools help the decision-makers understand the mined insight more than complex patterns in the data.

Decision Making: The visualized data aids in evidence-based decision-making. Business users can analyze the visual outputs for identifying trends, patterns, or anomalies that can drive the strategic actions.

5.3 Diagram representation of flow of Data Visualization

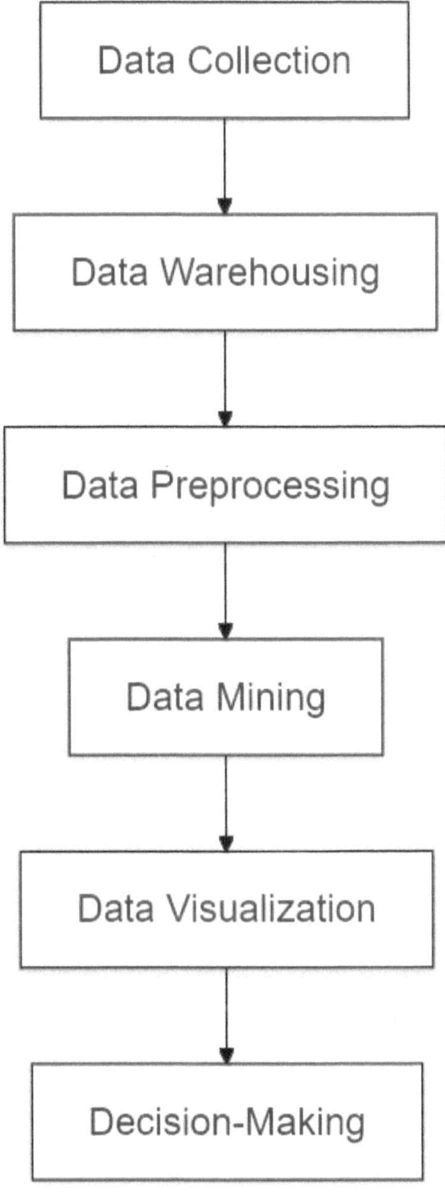

5.4 Importance of Data Visualization

Data visualization is important because it enhances the mostly complex and voluminous data into visuals that can be easily understood, analyzed, and acted on. In today's world, living through a period when data is increasingly becoming big and multi-dimensional in nature, raw numbers and statistics cannot be interpreted well.

Visualization tools like charts, graphs, heatmaps, and interactive dashboards simplify that complexity by showing data in a more attractive, intuitive, easy-to-understand form. It helps the user to notice trends, patterns, and anomalies more effectively than if they had to look into conventional tables of data, and allows for speedier and better-informed decision-making.

The importance goes even further, from making data available to improved communication and collaboration. Visually, it is able to take this very complex data set and turn it into a clear storyline that will provide better insights and mutual understanding among all participants at different levels of expertise.

Data visualization is an influential way of telling a story through data, whereby complex data is stitched in such a way that it forms a narrative that conveys meaningful insights to lead toward strategic choices. This form of storytelling does not only present clarity to the audience; instead, it makes the presentation more appealing, so the argument on data becomes convincing. That is why organizations started to act and innovate because they presented their data in such a way that was insightful yet inspiring. Data visualization, in other words, is crucial for making data actionable, improving communications, and driving better decisions strategically in today's data-driven environment.

5.5 Benefits of Data Visualization

Data visualization confers a host of benefits on the display and utilization of data in any field. **Better Comprehension:** The visual displays make complex data more comprehensible, bringing complicated relations and patterns into light that may well be obscured in raw data. The comprehension derived this way will assist in making appropriate decisions.

Faster Insights: More profound insights are gained from the visualizations by stakeholders without necessarily having to read through voluminous reports. This speed is important in dynamic environments where timely decisions could mean all the difference between a good and mediocre outcome.

Better Communication: Visuals are always more interesting and can simplify the message that otherwise would have been complicated to make people understand; hence, it's easier to communicate insights with people of different backgrounds. Due to this improved communication, collaboration can be done, and everyone in the team is on the same page as far as the data goes.

Trend and Pattern Visualization: Visualization tools make it easier to identify various trends, correlations, and anomalies in data. This is an important ability in terms of the determination of changes over time and what those changes might mean.

Data Storytelling: A great visualization tells a story in a way that leads audiences through the data and draws out the key messages. It does make the data more contextual and, therefore, more memorable.

Data Exploration: Interaction in visualization will enable viewers to explore information in real time, zoom in/out of detail, and look at data from multiple perspectives. The ability to explore will lead to deeper interaction with data.

Predictive Analytics: Visualization helps in identifying the historical trend that could drive forward-looking predictions. If organizations understand the pattern of the past, they might accurately forecast future performance or how their customers could behave.

Better Engagement: In most instances, other things being equal, visual information commands better attention than its text version. Engaging visuals let stakeholders take action or further investigate the data being presented.

Ease of Conception: Data visualization can be prepared for various levels of audiences. Even those who do not have great data literacy are able to understand the key concepts in the data. This democratization of data fosters a data-driven culture in organizations. Data visualization altogether enhances the skills of data interpretation and inference. It is also a systematic way to drive decision-making and stimulate collaboration.

5.6 Key Techniques in Data Visualization

A few key techniques in data visualization, serving the purpose of effectively communicating with better comprehension, are mentioned below.

Charts and Graphs: Bars, lines, pie graphs, scatter graphs, among others, are the very basic elements of data visualization. Different chart types fit different applications: comparing values, showing trends across time, or relationships between variables.

Sample Chart Types

Column Chart:

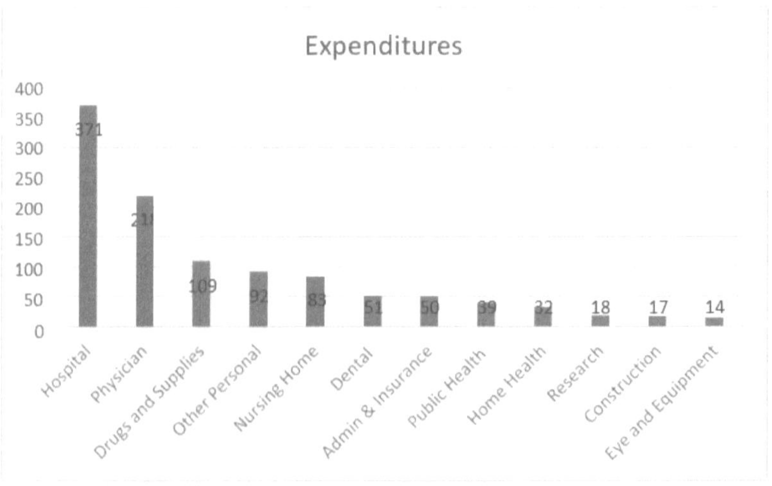

Line Chart

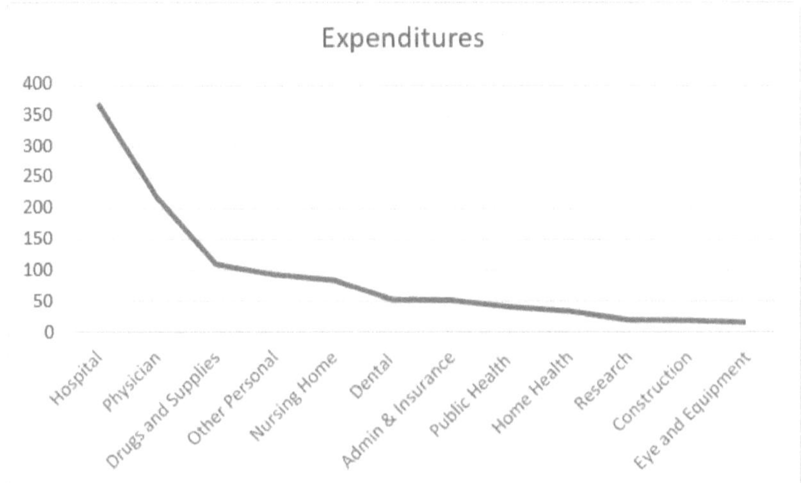

Pie Chart

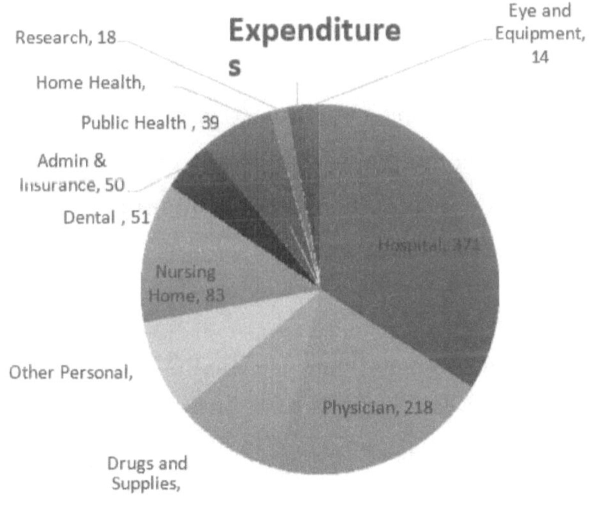

Scatter Chart

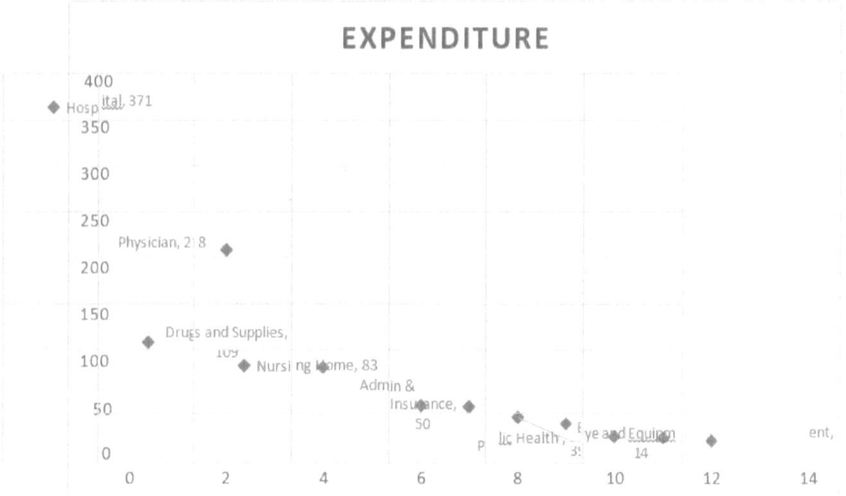

These charts reveal the expenditures incurred in different categories of health care.

Key Findings:

Highest Spending Hospital: It's clear from this that the largest number of expenditures occurs in the hospitals. That is, 371 units of such expenditure. This means that hospital services capture a large chunk of healthcare spending.

Major Categories

Doctor: The health provider with the second highest cost comes at 218 units representing doctor services. It reflects that doctors play a fundamental role in the health providers' system.

Drugs and Supplies: At 109 units drugs and supplies are also an expensive item where pharmaceutical constitutes part of the healthcare spending.

Other Personal: Expenditure here is 92 units which reflects a significant investment in personal care beyond the regular medical service.

Nursing Home: Nursing home care has 83 units, which also reflects an integral part of the healthcare spending.

Low Spending:

Categories such as Dental (51) and Admin & Insurance (50) portray balanced spending on prevention and office-expense terms.

Public Health (39) and Home Health (32) reflect lower spending that may reflect effectiveness in these or elsewhere a deficit in funding.

The research (18), construction (17), and eye and equipment categories evince the least amount of expense, implying that the least money is spent on these aspects compared to the direct care services.

In general, these charts give more emphasis to the provision of hospital and physician services in expenditure, focusing less attention towards dental care, public health, and research. Pragmatic importance is given to understanding these spending patterns as evidence for decision-making by stakeholders in the healthcare system to make more informed allocations regarding areas where investments might be increased or efficiency improved.

Dashboards: In a dashboard, several visualizations are combined into one interface for rapid views of **Key Performance Indicators (KPIs)** and metrics. They allow the user to monitor data in real time and gain valuable insights at a glance.

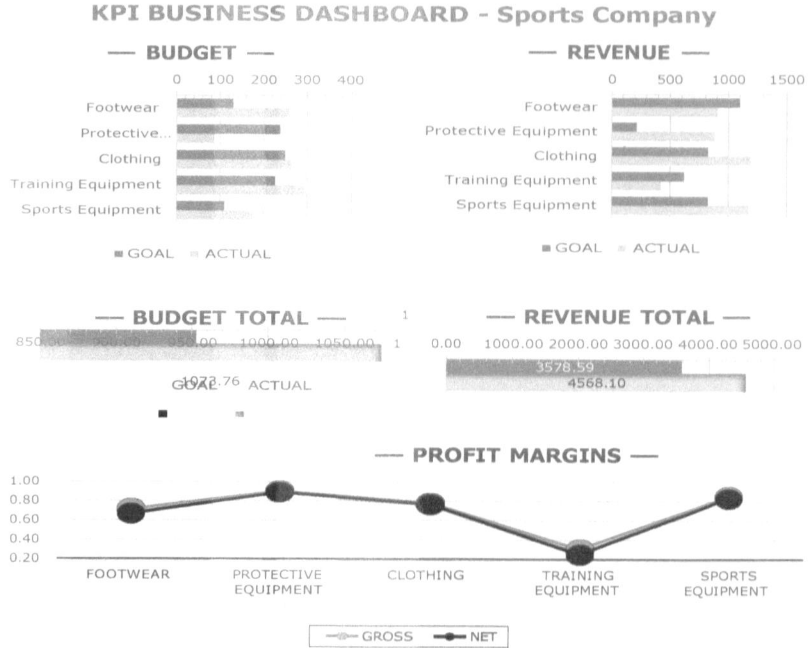

To effectively track and manage your business's performance, Key Performance Indicators (KPIs) such as budget, revenue, and profit margin are crucial metrics. Here's an outline of how they work together:

Budget: Planned financial allocation for income and expenses over a set period. Revenue: Total income generated from sales or services.

Profit Margin: Percentage of revenue remaining after all expenses are deducted.

Tracking these KPIs helps ensure financial health, strategic growth, and sustainable operations.

Geospatial Visualization: Geospatial visualization pertains to mapping data into geographic locations. Tools that help visualize such data include GIS. It assists in understanding how things relate to one another in space, like where the population is concentrated or where various resources are allocated.

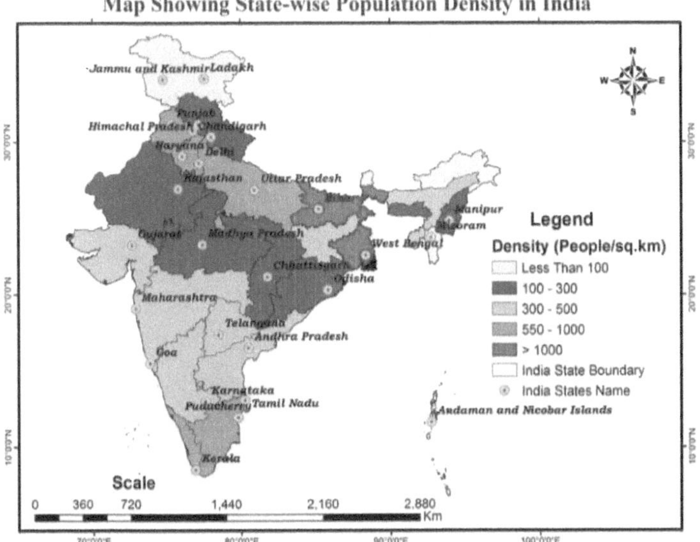

Interactive Visualization: It supplies users with an interface that interacts with the data through filtering, zooming, or drilling down further detail. This interactivity adds to the user experience and capabilities for further depth into the insight of the data.

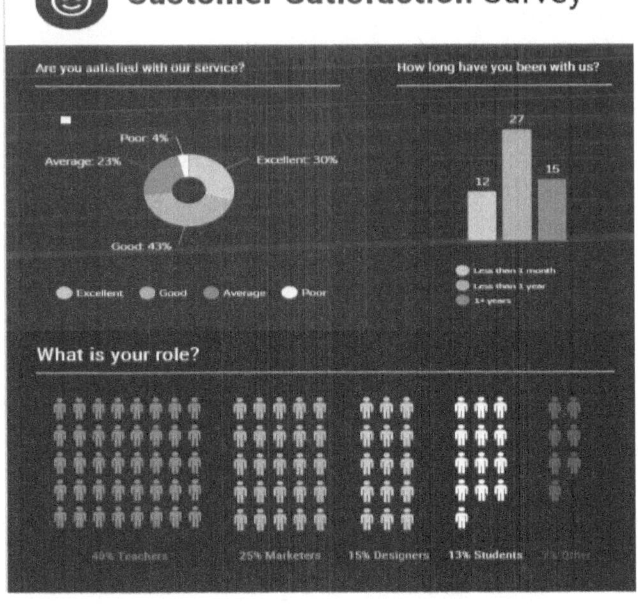

Time Series Analysis: This is the technique through which data points collected or recorded at regular periods are visualized. It majorly uses line graphs and area charts where the visualization of any trend that may be in occurrence over time thus capturing seasonality or

Cyclic Behavior:

Return over the period from July 2023 to June 2024.

Key Observations:

Overall Trend

The chart oscillates throughout the period and shows maximums and minimums clearly. The general range of the chart is between 294 and 307.

Monthly Highlights:

July 2023: Return starts with 294, a lowest point in the data.

August 2023: Large increase up to 305, moving upward.

September 2023: The return now drops back to 296, indicating this is a drawdown of sorts, at least for the time being.

October 2023: The return is steady at 300, which shows minimal fluctuation.

November 2023: A slight increase can be seen; once again, the return is at 305.

December 2023: The return dips back to 301, which shows minor fluctuations.

January 2024: The return increases to 307, which is the highest return ever recorded, thus showing a performance of strength.

February 2024: The return remains stable at 306, and that shows good consistent performance. March 2024: It goes back a bit to 304.

April 2024: It drops more significantly to 293, a lowest point since July 2023.

May 2024: The return continues falling to 298 which continues the decline pattern. June 2024: The return shoots back to 301 in a recovering pattern.

Volatility

There are some volatilities involved, especially in April and May 2024, where the return drops sharply.

Overall Recovery

The rebound indicates that during June 2024, recovery had been trending for the last month, following this pattern since showing a decline in April and May with an ending at 301-a drop from a high, though that was also in August and November. The return data displays a mix of stability and volatility across the year, along with extreme variations around the mean. The peak return happens in January 2024; July 2023 records the lowest return. Reversion observed in June 2024 will then indicate further scope for improvement, but returns as a whole remain to be observed carefully to draw conclusions and make decisions.

Box Plots: Box plots show the distribution of data based on minimum, first quartile, median, third quartile, and maximum. They are good to use when comparing the distribution of different groups.

The graph shows a "Quarterly Returns," with all returns in four quarters (Qtr1, Qtr2, Qtr3, and Qtr4).

Data Points: There is one point for each quarter that gives the average return marked with an

"X".

Error Bars: The horizontal lines extending from each "X" is the range or uncertainty in the data and gives the variability in returns for that quarter.

Trends

Qtr1: Average return appears to be around 895 with a particular range as reflected by the error bar.

Qtr2: Average return was more or less close to Qtr1 but was just a bit higher than that, around 905.

Qtr3: Return was similar to Qtr2 but tends to be just a bit higher on the same value. **Qtr4:** The average return is lower than that of Qtr3 and may be a small indication that the business or company might have done its worst or faced some decline in profitability or performance.

Interpretation: The quarterly return data did indicate some sort of fluctuation across the quarters, whereby the returns were stable during the second and third quarters but had lower values during the first and fourth quarters.

This chart helps in analyzing trends on financial performance over the quarters wherein the observed returns can help the stakeholders make decisions.

Network Diagrams: These visualizations express the association or network of data: examples would include social networks, organizational structures. They are good in bringing out complex associations and dependencies.

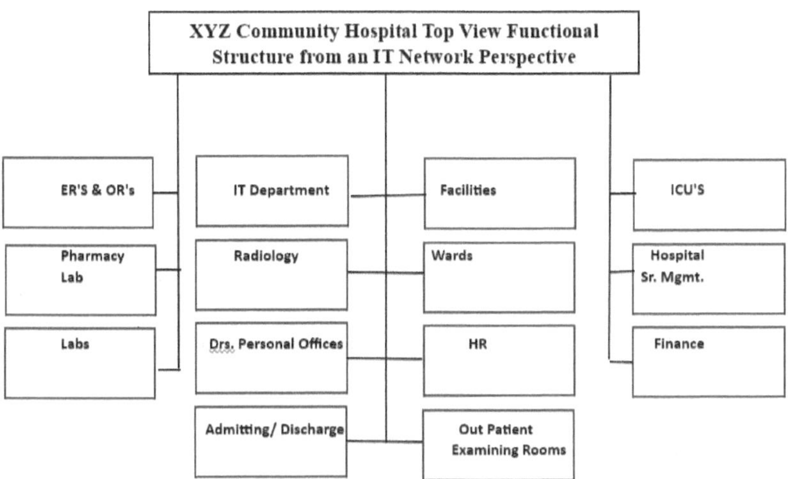

Storytelling with Data: This is the practice concerning the narrative of the data visualization itself, where an audience is taken through a series of insights in some form of logical order. Visuals underlying a story line make the information much more relatable and unforgettable.

These techniques enable data visualization to present complex information in an effective manner for comprehension and decision-making.

5.7 Tools for Data Visualization

There are numerous data visualization tools out there, each with unique features and capabilities that best fit different user needs and technical expertise.

5.8 Positive points of using tools for data visualization:

Improved Clarity: Simplifies complex data into easy-to-understand visuals. Faster Decision Making: Facilitates quicker insights for better business decisions. Enhanced Data Storytelling: Helps communicate data-driven stories effectively. Real-time Analysis: Provides up-to-date insights for dynamic decision-making.

User-friendly: Many tools are accessible to non-technical users, making data analysis more inclusive.

Customization: Offers the flexibility to tailor visuals to specific needs and audiences. Interactive Exploration: Enables users to interact with data for deeper insights.

Trend Identification: Makes it easier to spot patterns, trends, and anomalies in data.

Some of the popular ones used for data visualization are:

Tableau: Indeed, a powerful tool, Tableau possesses high-end functionality that enables users to build dynamic, shareable dashboards. It supports a wide variety of data sources and allows its users to create visualizations with a drag-and-drop feature.

Microsoft Power BI: It works effectively along with other Microsoft products, including robust data modeling, reporting, and visualization features. Power BI is relatively easy to use therefore, it can satisfy both beginners and advanced users.

Google Data Studio: A free tool that allows users to create interactive reports and dashboards using data from various Google services and other data sources. Its collaborative features enable easy sharing and real-time updates.

QlikView/Qlik Sense: At Qlik, the associates use its data instinctively. Qlik Sense is self-service, intuitive for the non-technical user, but equally from an advanced analytics perspective for data professionals.

D3.js: A JavaScript library to produce dynamic, interactive data visualizations for the web. D3.js is a very extensible library, enabling developers to create complex visualizations specific to their needs.

R and ggplot2: R is a programming language that is very popular for doing statistical processing; ggplot2 is one of the powerful visualization packages in R that allows for advanced and customized visualizations based on the grammar of graphics.

Python with Matplotlib and Seaborn: Python is also one of the most famous programming languages for data analysis and data visualization. While Matplotlib is a multi-purpose library that targets the creation of static, animated, and interactive plots, Seaborn extends Matplotlib to provide a higher-level interface for drawing attractive and informative statistical graphics.

Excel: General-purpose data analysis and visualization tool. It includes a range of charting options and other functionality useful in the construction of basic visualizations. It is relatively easy to use by the casual user and fits well into the greater set of Microsoft Office products.

Looker: Data exploration and visualization platform that includes tools to build and share interactive dashboards. With Looker, users can build custom visualizations and get insights from their data.

Each of these is good to go for different use cases, whether business intelligence, academic research, or personal projects, since each shine in its own ways. Many times, the kind of tool you will need is dictated by specific requirements, data sources, and user expertise.

5.9 Challenges in Data Visualization

Data visualization produces a host of challenges that can impact one's effectiveness in communicating insights. A few of the most important are described below.

Data Quality: Poor data quality can lead to visualizations that are not accurate. Partial data, inconsistent data, or data that is outdated distorts trends and relationships within the data, thus corroding credibility around the analysis.

Overcomplication: Most users face the problem of visual overload or overcomplication. Overloading a visualization with too much complication of data points or embellishments can confuse the audience instead of providing clarity on insights.

Misleading Visuals: A badly scaled axis, inappropriate chart type, or wrong color may distort the message and lead to misinterpretation. It's time for assurance that the visuals depict data accurately.

Understanding the Audience: The various sections of the audience are pretty different in terms of data literacy and their familiarity with various methods of visualization. As a matter of fact, this is one of the challenges in designing the visuals that would be suited to each type of audience.

Limitations of Tools: The functionality, customizability, or integrability-the features on offer in data visualization tools-run from a very low to a very high level, indeed, with many options available. It is tough to choose which one will fit the particular need.

Interactivity Issues: Interactive visualizations may increase engagement but at times cause confusion if it is not intuitively designed. Often, working one's way through complicated interactions and knowing how to manipulate data is quite hard for users.

Each of these pitfalls requires a reasoned approach to the design, engagement with an understanding of the audience, and devotion to integrity of the data. The best preparation for a practitioner to construct effective and powerful visualizations is having an awareness of such pitfalls.

5.10 Future Trends in Data Visualization

Data visualization continuously evolves either with the use of technology or change in user needs. Some of the main trends in data visualization for times to come are given as under:

More AI and Machine Learning: Artificial Intelligence and machine learning algorithms will slowly be inserted into data visualization software as a way to automatically find insights and build predictive visualizations. These technologies will finally give the user a much better way of finding patterns and trends within large datasets with much higher efficiency.

Engaging and Immersive Visualization: Augmented and virtual reality for information visualization finds its momentum in the present times. These devices basically empower users to interact with data in three-dimensional environments, thus enabling them to get deeper insights with increasing user interactions.

Real-time data visualization: As the demand for real-time analytics increases, the support of data visualization tools for live feeds will allow users to monitor metrics and KPIs in motion. This will enhance decision-making in fast-paced environments.

Self-Service BI Tools: Today, the trend is to move towards self-service BI, in which non- technical users have been able to develop their own visualizations and dashboards without IT intervention. Such democratization of access encourages a data-driven culture in the organizations.

Data Storytelling: There will be an increasing priority on data storytelling-where, through visualizations, it conveys a story in setting the data into context. In this way, the audience would understand what the implication of the data was and thus engage them.

Personalization of Visualizations: The capabilities for personalization will be seen in forthcoming data visualization tools that will enable each user to personalize their dashboards or reports according to their taste or organizational roles.

Cloud-based visualization solutions: With increasing momentum, cloud computing is embracing the notion of collaborative data visualization. By using cloud-based tools, users can simultaneously access, share, and edit visualizations to further enhance the collaboration and sharing aspects of data.

NLP Integration: As NLP applications allow the user to query the data in a natural way, it therefore, reduces barriers in making visualizations and gaining insights without the technical knowledge.

Mobile-Friendly Visualizations: As mobile devices start becoming much more common as a means of accessing data, the focus will increasingly shift towards developing responsive, mobile-friendly visualizations.

As data visualization continues to evolve, these trends will define how organizations and people make meaning out of data and communicate insight toward smarter decisions and a data-driven culture.

5.11 Conclusion

Data visualization has become one of the key components in today's data landscape. it transforms complex data into understandable and insightful visualizations. In addition, its importance is underlined by its capabilities in enhancing understanding, facilitating faster decision-making, and improving communication across diverse audiences. With this, we can expect exciting trends in the integration of artificial intelligence, immersive visualization experience, and real-time analytics that will further empower users toward actionable insights from   data.

However, best practices in visualization need to be ensured by overcoming data quality, complexity, and interpretation by the audience. Equipped with continuous updates on best practices and a feeling for new trends, organizations can ensure data visualization activates strategy, unites teams, and injects a data culture into the very fabric of the company. Eventually, living in a world of accumulating data, the approach of data presentation will remain an important tool in unlocking the potential of data and making decisions in many spheres.

5.12 Data Visualization in Finance: Overview

Financial data visualization helps an analyst or professional in extracting meaningful information out of complex financial data, which in turn can help in decision-making. The same information is further communicated for maximum impact. The importance and uses of data visualization are elaborated below in detail:

5.13 Importance of Data Visualization in Finance

Smarter decision-making: Financial experts lean on data visualization to make decisions by drawing from fast insights. Visualizing financial metrics, trends, and forecasts essentially equips analysts and managers with the capability to understand at an instance the current levels of financial health and the current market condition.

Risk Management: Through visual tools, it becomes easier to identify and measure the financial risks by just drawing a line on trends and anomalies. The level of exposure, potential threat, along with the respective consequences for different risk factors, can be shown on the dashboard.

Investment Analytics: Investors use data visualization while analyzing stock performance, market trends, and portfolio diversification. It helps them to take a call on an investment opportunity with the use of candlestick charts, scatter plots, and trend lines.

Regulatory Compliance: Through the use of visualizations, financial regulations are more easily met with clarity and precision in presenting data that required for reporting. This can include financial statements, audit trails, and compliance metrics.

5.14 Visualization Techniques

Line Charts: These are used for monitoring financial metrics, such as stock prices, revenue trends, and economic indicators, over-time.

Bar Charts: Comparing financial figures across different quarters of the year, or comparing budget allocation across several departments, is easier.

Pie Charts: Good to illustrate the percentage of various components contributing to a whole, such as the distribution of market share or the categories of expenses.

Candlestick Charts: These are widely applied in trading to represent the movement of prices over time and show the opening, high, low, and closing prices for stocks or other types of financial instruments.

Bubble Charts: They serve to visualize a relationship between three variables- for instance, investment risk, return, and market size.

Line Chart

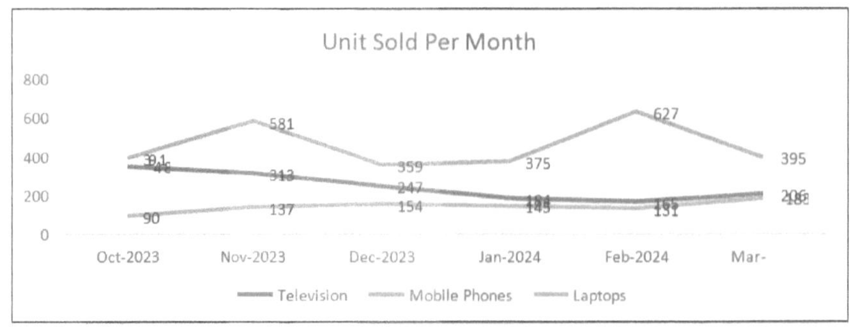

Bar Chart

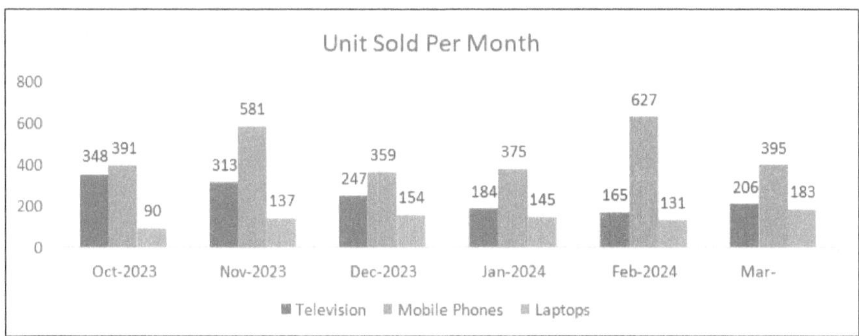

Pie Chart

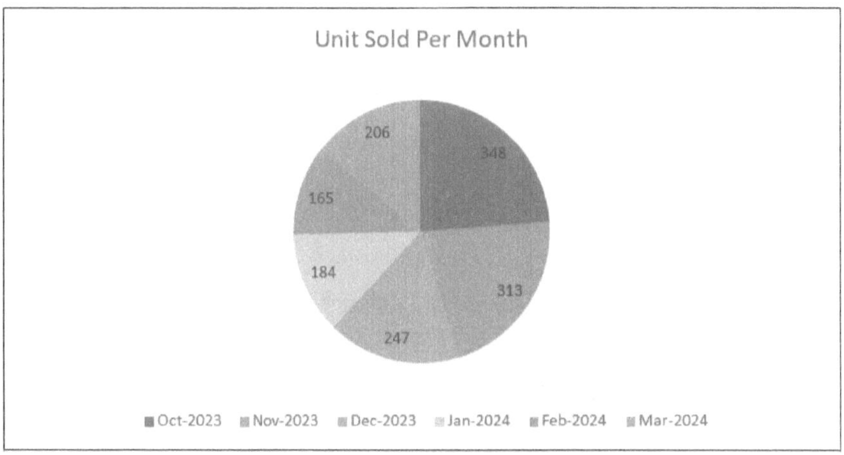

5.14 Common Tools of Data Visualization in Finance

Following are the few common data visualizing tools in finance:

Tableau: This is one of the most well-known data visualization tools that allow users to create interactive dashboards and visualizations from various sources. Tableau is quite popular because it is pretty easy to use and can be utilized on large amounts of data.

Microsoft Power BI: This is a business intelligence software that offers advanced visualization capability to create interactive reports and dashboards.

Power BI has inbuilt integrations with many other Microsoft applications and is, therefore, the crowd-pleaser among financiers.

Excel: Although Excel is a spreadsheet application, it does offer several ways of data visualization, like chart and graph creation and pivot tables. Most people in finance use Excel for fast analysis and visualization since this application is well known and accessible.

QlikView/Qlik Sense: Qlik's tool suite offers intuitive associative data modeling that enables users to intuitively explore and analyze financial data. These platforms support interactive dashboards and self-service analytics-attributes that explain their popularity in financial analysis.

D3.js: A very powerful JavaScript library with capabilities for dynamic and interactive visualization within web browsers. D3.js provides extensive options for customizing visualizations. It is truly capable of creating tailored financial visualizations.

R with ggplot2: R is a statistical programming language very popular among finance. Ggplot2 is a package in this environment, which allows developing complex, visually attractive visualizations based on the grammar of graphics.

Python with Matplotlib and Seaborn: The use of Python is also gaining momentum within data analysis and visualization in finance. Libraries like Matplotlib and Seaborn provide full- fledged possibilities for both static and interactive visualizations.

Looker: A platform for the exploration and visualization of data, enabling users to build customized reports and dashboards. Because Looker supports a broad array of data sources, and its views are real-time, it serves financial applications rather well.

Infogram: Without requiring deep design experience from finance professionals, Infogram is simple to use, featuring a set of ready templates and drag-and-drop functions.

MicroStrategy: This is a business intelligence platform that provides advanced analytics and visualization on financial data. MicroStrategy is known for its enterprise scalability and features.

Sisense: Business Intelligence tool to empower users with analyzing and visualizing any type of data from any source in any format. Sisense is recognized for powerful data modeling and analytics capabilities, thus fit for financial applications.

They come with different features and functionalities that are helpful for financial professionals to better visualize complex data, track performance, and support informed decisions.

5.16 Challenges in Financial Data Visualization

Data Integration: Integration of data from different sources such as market feeds, financial reports, and economic indicators can be very tricky and requires quality tools and methodologies.

Accuracy and Precision: Accuracy and precision in visualizations remain literally key because just a little mistake may further lead to misguided decisions.

User Experience: The development of visualizations shall provide informative yet user- friendly views. Financial users should easily interact with visualizations and understand the information portrayed.

5.17 Future of Financial Data Visualization

Advanced Analytics: AI and Machine learning can be incorporated to perform predictive analytics and also allow for automated insights.

Interactive Dashboards: There can be a greater focus on utilizing dynamic interactive elements on dashboards, enabling users to explore views and create personalized views to meet their needs.

Real-time Visualization: Increasing demand for real-time visualization of data to monitor market conditions and financial metrics on the go.

Personalization in Reporting: More personalization of reporting and visualization in finance, tailoring for different user preferences and roles.

In other words, Data Visualization is the key tool of the financial sector that helps analyze and make decisions on finances more qualitatively, or even communicate financial information. As technology and complexity keep developing with time, techniques and tools for visualizing finances do, too, which allows driving continued innovation and efficiency in the industry.

Chapter 6

Database Management Systems (DBMS)

6.1 Introduction

A Database Management System could be described as a complex application program which is designed uniquely for proper definition, creation, control, and management with the main objective being the manipulation of access to databases hence ensuring proper retrieval of organization and storage of data. The DB user can store data through the database interface in a structured manner. In the conventional, general form, a systematic arrangement and manipulation of data are done in a table and in the form of relationships which can be easily queried and manipulated. It does support the integrity of data via a set of rules and constraints that help in preserving the accuracy and consistency of the information that has been stored.

A DBMS also takes care of other complex functionalities, such as transaction management, which assures that several operations on the database have been done in an appropriate and safe manner so as to maintain the properties of Atomicity, Consistency, Isolation, Durability (ACID). It also provides functionality control that allows users to access the database at the same point in time without conflicting actions. Also, it provides strong security features for the data against unauthorized access and facilities to back up and recover so that no data is lost. The DBMS is, therefore, significant in today's data-centric applications, providing support for an array of fields to manage the bundles of data swiftly through an abstraction of how data is stored and providing a well-situated interface.

History and Evolution: The history and evolution of Database Management Systems (DBMS) dates back to the early 1960s, when the storage solutions were purely file-based and worked without a formal database structure. These systems were heavy since, at the time that followed, they did not have features to effectively handle the much data neither support multi-users. Siegert 1966 saw the first major breakthrough through the hierarchical database model specifically IBM's Information Management System (IMS). Hierarchal databases represented data in a tree-like structure and although quite efficient for some purposes were really very inflexible and simplistic in general. The shortcomings of these models eventually led to the development of the network model in the late sixties, led by the CODASYL group. Second, the graph-connected structure that supported more complex relationships among data was provided for in the IMS while remaining less user-friendly.

The true breakthrough occurred in the 1970s with the idea of the relational database model being developed by Dr. Edgar F. Codd, an IBM researcher.

Still, the relational model was what actually changed the very outlook on data handling; it was much more intuitive, flexible, and mathematically grounded than the previous ones. Structured Query Language, SQL, developed at the end of the 1970s, turned into the established and effective means for developing applications that browse, search, and update information stored in RDBMS. During the 1980s and 1990s, there was an explosion of commercial relational DBMS products—for example, Oracle, IBM DB2, Microsoft SQL Server—offering ever more sophisticated features.

It's the sophistication of the traditional relational databases that has weaknesses in handling unstructured data and scaling horizontally into a distributed system, which gave birth to something—NoSQL databases—in the late years of the 20th and early years of the 21st centuries.

Working with these is the range of document-oriented, column-family, key-value, and graph databases specifically built to fulfil the many types of data requirements that modern applications have, particularly in a web and big data context. In parallel with that, the dawn of cloud computing introduced Database as a Service in which a cloud provider takes responsibility for maintaining database infrastructure, greatly easing the burden of deploying and scaling databases. DBMS has continued to evolve even today and integrates into newly emerging technologies like AI, machine learning with blockchain and also adapts in the growing needs of data analytic tools in big data, real-time processing, and big data analytic tools in global distribution.

Importance of DBMS: Database Management Systems (DBMS) plays a very important role in the management of data efficiently in almost all the sectors of the modern economy.

They therefore play a very pivotal role in ensuring structured and secure storing, retrieving and manipulation of data. A DBMS is however important in the sense that it provides a central framework in which various users can interact with data simultaneously without affecting its integrity. This is because DBMS organizes data into structured formats; therefore, there is reduced redundancy and increased consistency of applications. On the other hand, data storage by a DBMS is also secured through access control and encryption, which protect sensitive information from unauthorized access and any possible leakage. It also guarantees data integrity by enforcing rules and constraints that ensure accuracy and reliability, and it has mechanisms for backup and recovery to ensure that the data can be restored in the case of system failure. Moreover, by abstracting away from the complexity of the data management workload, DBMS can enable concentration on application development and decision-making by the user or developer without any concerns for the processes involved in the storage and management of data underneath.

Application of DBMS: Due to versatility and effectiveness in managing data, DBMS finds applications in diverse industries. A few important ones include:

Banking and Finance: DBMS is applied vastly in the banking sector. Customer information, transactions, loans, and credit cards are all managed through DBMS. It supports real-time processing; thereby, the financial transaction time is shortened and at the same time, records of all the activities are maintained.

Healthcare: DBMS in healthcare is used to maintain records of patient registration, treatment history, various medical images, and billing information. This is important in making it easier to retrieve the patient's data for proper care and management of the hospital.

Retail and E-commerce: DBMS forms the core operational unit for most retail businesses, specifically inventory, customer orders, and transaction records. E-commerce platforms use DBMS to maintain customer purchase records and the product lifecycle, which helps businesses offer personalized shopping experiences and manage supply chains properly.

Education: In educational institutions, DBMS is used for maintaining records of students, course registrations, grades, and scheduling. Quite simply, the system helps to make educational administration smoother through the much easier access and updating of information by educators and administrators.

Telecommunications: A very large amount of data is maintained by DBMS in the telecommunications sector regarding customer accounts, call records, billing, and management of networks. It helps to facilitate the speedy and efficient handling of customer queries and billing processes as well as analyze network usage.

Government: Governments use DBMS to administer huge forms of data that range right from the kinds of information received from censuses, taxation records, and voter registrations to the data of social services. It helps them in timely public service provisions and managing large databases.

Manufacturing: The manufacturing operations utilize DBMS for managing supply chain information, manufacturing schedules, and inventory levels.

It supports just-in-time production processes that enable the optimum use of resources.

Social media and Networking: DBMS aids social media websites in the management of their users' profiles, posts, messages, and their respective interactions. This data can further be used for delivering suitable content to users, managing user relationships, and extracting social trends.

Travel and Tourism: DBMS is in the core of handling bookings, customer details, flight schedules, hotel reservations, and travel schedule itinerary details. This can help in managing resources efficiently and providing updated information to customers.

These are a few examples of the vast, far-reaching applicability of DBMS in any industry and also show how DBMS serves as the foundation for data-driven decision-making, operational efficiency, and innovation.

Database Models

The database models of a DBMS define the way data is organized, stored, and accessed. A few database models are in existence, and a couple of them are unique:

Hierarchical Model: Probably the earliest model, it presents the data in a tree structure for which every record has one parent and might have many children. This model is suitable when the application in question has a high level of hierarchy, but it does tend to be less flexible in terms of handling complex relationships.

Network Model: An extension of the hierarchical model that develops much more complex relationships between records by supporting many-to-many relationships. It organizes data as graph nodes and edges, giving more flexibility at the cost of added complexity in data management.

Relational Model: Probably the most common these days, a relational model organizes data into tables with rows, records and column attributes.

Data integrity is maintained, and it is manipulated using SQL. Very high use is because it is simple, flexible, and has a mathematical foundation; therefore, it is very powerful, and so appropriate for a large number of applications.

Object-Oriented Model: This model is a combination of database capabilities and the principles of object-oriented programming. Data is stored in this model like the objects that are manipulated by programming languages. It supports complex data types, inheritance, and encapsulation; hence, it is appropriate for applications that require advanced and intricate relationships among the data.

Comparison Summary

Feature	Hierarchical Model	Network Model	Relational Model	Object-Oriented Model
Data Structure	Tree (one-to-many)	Graph (many-to- many)	Table (relations)	Objects (classes and inheritance)
Flexibility	Low	Moderate	High	High
Complex Relationships	Hard to represent	Easier than hierarchical	Uses joins to establish relationships	Easily supports complex types (inheritance, polymorphism)
Ease of Use	Hard to modify or query	Complex navigation	Easy with SQL	Requires understanding of OOP concepts
Efficiency	Efficient for hierarchical data	Efficient for predefined relationships	Scales well but can be slower with complex joins	Suitable for data complex operations
Standardization	Not standardized	Not standardized	SQL standard	Limited standardization, but gaining traction

DBMS Architecture

Mostly, the architecture of a Database Management System (DBMS) is tri-level: internal level, conceptual level, and external level, and therefore, it is referred to commonly as the three-level architecture.

Internal Level: This level is also known as the level of storage; it is the lowest level at which data in the database is stored. It describes how the data is normally physically stored in regard to storage blocks, indexing, and access methods, maintaining a lot of efficiency and making everything at the storage level make sense in regard to storage.

Conceptual Level: This is sometimes known as the logical level by which it presents a unified view of the entire database, irrespective of the way data is physically stored. It is the level to establish characteristics or properties of the data and the relationship between data and to put in place constraints, ensuring the consistency and integrity of data.

External Level: This topmost level, also known as the view level, is the level that interacts with the users and explains how each single user views his or her data. It can be the case wherein the users would like to view different versions of the same database with a different interface and access rights based on his role and requirements.

The three-tier architecture ensures data abstraction and independence; changes at each level are carried out without adjusting the other levels—for example, storage methods are changed at the internal level, and the other two levels are not affected. This makes it flexible and effective to manage databases.

Database Schema and Independence

A Database Schema is a blueprint that defines the structure and organization of data within a database.

In simple terms, it is the organization of data in the form of a table, indicating the relationships among them while showing the data type to be used in every column. A schema defines tables, columns, indexes, constraints, views, and other database objects as may exist on a database. It is the plan that guides the building of the database—the blueprint through which the stored data can be structured and accessed.

It manages the three schemas generally in the DBMS: **logical schema** that describes the logical structure—for example, tables and relationships, physical **schema** that details the actual storage of the data on the hardware, such as file systems and **external schema**, which describes the manner in which data is presented to different groups of users or applications. With this clear structuring, the database schema ensures data consistency, integrity, and efficient retrieval and management.

Data Independence says that it is possible to change the schema definition in a specific database level without changing the schema definition at the next higher level. This concept becomes very important in a Database Management System, providing flexibility in the design and maintenance of the database. Data independence is of two types:

Logical Data Independence: A capability to change the logical schema with regard to modification of tables or relationships, for example, yet not having to change the user views or the external schema at the same time. This means that the mode of interaction with the data is not changed even if the structure of the database is changed.

Physical Data Independence: The ability to change a physical schema or scheme used for storing data on the disk without affecting the logical schema. It means that the change of structures of storage or hardware configurations won't imply that the application's code needs to be changed.

Data independence is critical for the long-term application maintainability and scalability of databases in a system, as it lessens the need for having numerous rewrites and updates just to effect changes.

Overview of Relational Database Management Systems

This is a type of database management system that is modelled to collect and manage data in a row-column structured order.

Developed from the relational model introduced in the 1970s by Edgar F. Codd, RDBMS stores data in tables, also called relations, in which each row represents a record and each column represents an attribute. According to the relational model, primary keys identify records in a table, and a foreign key is a construct to draw connections between tables. These concepts enable effective practice in managing complex data structures that might be countable but time- consuming without them.

An RDBMS is SQL-centric. It sets down a standard way in which data structures, questions to the database for data, and data manipulation, other than inserting, updating, and deleting data, are written. The relational model enforces the integrity of data mainly through means of constraints- primary keys provide uniqueness, foreign keys provide referential integrity, and check constraints deal with further issues of validity.

Some of the important features of RDBMS include normalization, which means organizing data with an attempt to reduce redundancy and provide more integrity to the data by dividing the data into related tables. This would help to avoid inconsistency and anomalies in the handling of the data. RDBMSs also follow the properties of ACID: atomicity, consistency, isolation, and durability, ensuring reliable transactions and data integrity with system failures or concurrent transactions.

RDBMSs have become very common in many applications, including financial systems, enterprise resource planning (ERP) systems, customer relationship management (CRM) systems), etc. due to their robustness, ease of use, capability of managing complex queries, and data relationships. They provide a robust way to manage structured data with high flexibility, making them the backbone for modern data management and analytics.

RDBMS Design

Database design holds one of the crucial stages in designing a well-structured, and efficient database system. Involving schema of the database included, which data will be stored, how data elements will carry a relationship with each other, and rules and guidelines will be required for constraining to ensure to carry data with integrity. The designing of any database lay in a conceptual design which is modelled initially where different tools like Entity-Relationship (ER) define all the entities, attributes, and the relationship among them. This is followed by the logical design, which translates the conceptual model into a relational schema comprising tables, columns, and keys. Finally, the physical design involves optimization of the database schema for performance and storage. Considering aspects like indexing and partitioning, effective database design ensures data is organized in a manner that supports efficient query, maintains data consistency, and is appropriate to meet the requirements of the application.

Normalization

Normalization is the practice that database designers follow in the organization of data to reduce duplication, and increase data integrity.

This is basically the dissection of a database in several tables and the establishing of relationships between them: all this follows a series of rules or "normal forms." The key objectives are the sure logical storage of data and fields and making any updates, deletions, or insertions without leading to any anomaly. There are usually a number of steps, such as First Normal Form (1NF), which reduces redundancy by making sure that each column contains atomic values; Second Normal Form (2NF), which eliminates partial dependencies by ensuring that non-key attributes are fully functionally dependent on the primary key; and Third Normal Form, which eliminates transitive dependencies by ensuring that non-key attributes are only dependent upon the primary key. Normalization tends to make the process of the underlying database efficient, flexible, and maintainable.

Denormalization

Denormalization intentionally adds some sort of redundancy in the database design with due cause, but it does it to increase performance. This basically involves increasing query efficiency and speed. Unlike normalization, which tries to minimize data redundancy and maintain data integrity through a series of normal forms, denormalization could involve the combination of tables or include redundant data to optimize read-heavy operations. This trade-off can reduce the complexity of queries and thus the number of joins, thereby increasing the rate at which the data is obtained. The disadvantage of denormalization occurs in increasing data anomalies and requiring more mechanisms to take care of consistency and update handling. It is generally used in circumstances when the increased speed obtained by a clearer query is greater than the good normative of the structure of the database.

Structured Query Language (SQL)

SQL is a programming language type that is specifically used to manage and communicate relational database systems.

SQL is the generalized interface through which queries are written, data updates are submitted, and management functions are performed in a DBMS system. It allows users to retrieve data with SELECT statements, change the data with INSERT, UPDATE, and DELETE statements, and define the structure of a database via CREATE, ALTER, and DROP statements. This means that SQL presents a standard means of communication with the DBMS, simplifies complex data manipulations, maintains data integrity and security, and allows fast and easy data fetching and processing. Its declarative nature allows users to specify what data they need without detailing how to retrieve it, making database interactions more intuitive and powerful.

Basic SQL Commands

Data Definition Language (DDL): Data Definition Language (DDL) refers to a subset of SQL statement used to define or modify the structure of database objects like tables, indexes, schemas. Here are the examples of DDL commands:

CREATE

Purpose: Define table, view, other objects of database.

Syntax:

CREATE TABLE table_name (column1 datatype constraints, column2 datatype constraints,….);

Other Uses: CREATE INDEX: to create index to enhance query performance. CREATE INDEX index_name ON table_name (column_name);

CREATE VIEW: to create virtual table based on a query.

CREATE VIEW view_name 1 AS SELECT column1, column2 FROM table_name b. WHERE condition;

ALTER

Purpose: Modify the structure of an existing database object

Syntax:

ALTER TABLE table_name ADD column_name datatype constraints;

Other Uses:

ALTER TABLE: Drop, alter or change the columns, and modify the data type or change the name of the table

ALTER TABLE table_name MODIFY column_name datatype; ALTER TABLE table_name DROP COLUMN column_name; ALTER TABLE table_name RENAME TO new_table_name; **DROP**

Purpose: Remove existing database objects.

Syntax:

DROP TABLE table_name;

Other Uses:

DROP INDEX: Remove an index from a table. DROP INDEX index_name;

DROP VIEW: Drop the view from a database. DROP VIEW view_name;

Summary

CREATE: Create new database objects. ALTER: Modify existing database objects. DROP: Remove existing database objects.

DDL commands are most useful for designing and maintaining the schema. Applications require a structure based on business requirements.

Data Manipulation Language (DML) SQL supports a DML, or a data manipulation language, that allows you to manipulate and maintain the contents of database tables. The main commands of DML are:

SELECT

Purpose: Retrieve information from one or multiple tables.

Syntax:

SELECT column1, column2 …. FROM table_name WHERE condition;

Additional Clauses:

ORDER BY: Sorts the result set.

SELECT column1, column2 FROM table_name ORDER BY column1 ASC|DESC; GROUP BY: Groups rows which have identical values.

SELECT column1, COUNT (*) FROM table name GROUP BY column1; HAVING: Filters on grouped rows based on a condition.

SELECT column1, COUNT (*) FROM table name GROUP BY column1 HAVING COUNT(*) > value;

INSERT INTO

Purpose: Build new rows in a table.

Syntax:

INSERT INTO table name VALUES(value1, value2…);

UPDATE

Purpose: Modifying records in a table

UPDATE table name SET column1 = value1, column2 = value2, . WHERE condition;

Important: The WHERE clause specifies which record(s) that should be updated. If you omit the WHERE clause, all record will be updated.

DELETE

Purpose: Removing rows from a table

Syntax:

DELETE FROM table name WHERE condition;

Important Note: Similar to UPDATE, you specify a WHERE clause that says which rows to remove or you will be removing all rows from the table.

Summary

SELECT: Retrieve data from one or more tables INSERT INTO: Add new rows to a table UPDATE: Modify exist records

DELETE: Remove rows from a table

DML statements such as INSERT and UPDATE are the basic means of retrieving and manipulating information residing in a relational database.

Data Control Language (DCL): It is an important part of SQL that helps in controlling data access. Some DCL commands include user permission control in a database and database security. Given below is an elaborated introduction to the different types of important DCL commands:

GRANT

It provides some particular type of permission to a user or role for doing something with a database object. The syntax of the GRANT command is:

GRANT privilege-type ON object-type(object-name) TO user-name;

There are several types for privilege type, like for example, SELECT, UPDATE, DELETE, and so on.

INSERT: Add new rows into a table UPDATE: Modifies existing in a table DELETE: Remove the rows from a table ALL: All the privileges available

REVOKE

Purpose: Reverses existing privileges from users or roles.

Syntax:

REVOKE privilege type ON object type object name FROM user or role;

Privileges: Almost same as those granted, can have SELECT: Revoke read privilege

INSERT: Revoke privilege to add row UPDATE: Revoke privilege to modify data DELETE: Revoke privilege to remove row ALL: Revoke all privileges

Summary

GRANT: Give or hand out particular permissions to specific users or roles.

REVOKE: This command is used to take back access rights of specified users or roles from the specified resources.

Database security is a main reason why DCL commands are really essential; it is vital to administer the right level of access that will be provided to the user for the data.

Transactions and Concurrency Control

Transactions are one or more SQL operations executed as a single unit of work. A transaction guarantees that a certain series of operations in a database run completely and with success. In an event a portion of the transaction fails, the roll-back concept comes into place and ensures data integrity.

ACID Properties

Following are the ACID properties adhered to by the transactions to provide reliability and consistency to the operations of databases:

Atomicity: Stating that all the operations included in a transaction must be either carried out fully or undone fully in case of failure by any single operation. If one part fails, then the whole transaction fails. As a result, the database remains unchanged.

Consistency: It is the property by which a transaction takes a database from one consistent state to another. At the beginning and end of any transaction, the integrity constraints and business rules are maintained.

Isolation: It gives a feeling that the concurrent transactions are not affecting each other. While executing concurrent transactions, every transaction behaves as if it is the only transaction that is running in the system.

Durability: Once a transaction is committed, the changes made by it are permanently saved in the database. The means—however adverse the condition of a system failure may be—its impact will be persistent.

Isolation Levels

Isolation levels determine how isolated each operation of a single transaction is from operations of other concurrent transactions. Major isolation levels are:

Read Uncommitted: The weakest isolation level in which transactions read data that has not yet been committed by other transactions. A dirty read occurs when one transaction reads other's uncommitted values, which could lead to inconsistency.

Read Committed: This ensures that transactions can only read those data that have already been committed by other transactions. It prevents dirty reads but does allow non-repeatable reads; data may change if read again within the same transaction.

Repeatable Read: Guarantees that, if a transaction reads any data item, it will get the same value if it accesses that item again later in the transaction. It does not prevent phantom reads, which means that new rows might appear or disappear.

Serializable: This is the highest isolation level that gives full isolation by making transactions appear fully serial. It prevents dirty, non-repeatable, and phantom reads but can greatly hamper the performance because of the strict control.

These principles of transaction and concurrency control help in managing data integrity and consistency.

Data Security and Integrity

Data Security refers to steps and actions in place to protect information from unauthorized access, breaches, or corruption. Data security can be broken down into strategies and technologies from when the datum is created until when it is finally archived and or destroyed. The principal elements of data security are as follows:

Authentication: This means identity verification for users or systems accessing the database. The typical methods are used are traditional password methods, multi-factor authentication, and biometric verification.

Authorization: Authorization is the amount of access and permissions allowed to authenticated users; it basically determines what actions a user can perform on or with the data. It is a definition of roles, which come with specific privileges that allow or deny access to particular database objects and operations.

Encryption: The process protects data into a format that is unreadable without the proper decryption key. It protects both stored data, which is data at rest, and data moving across networks, which is data in transit.

Monitoring and auditing: This entails finding and recording every activity carried out in the database so that cases of any unauthorized access and anomalies are detected and remedied. In great detail, the access attempts, changes concerning the data and the events in the system are recorded for further analysis and compliance measures.

Data Integrity: Data Integrity is a term that is used to define the accuracy, consistency, and reliability of data over its complete lifecycle. Data that has integrity is valid and accurate. A couple of the key elements of data integrity will include:

Constraints: These are a set of rules applied to data to assure the validity of the data. Typical types of constraints will include:

Primary Key: This enables us to guarantee that all the records in a table are unique and uniquely identifiable.

Foreign Key: Works to keep the referential integrity by proving that a value in one table has a correspondence with a value in another table.

Unique Constraint: Makes sure that all values of a column are different within the database.

Check constraint: It imposes specific conditions on the values of a column.

Normalization: It is used to package data within the database in a way that reduces redundancy and improves the data integrity. The concept involves dividing the data in relevant tables and ensuring that relationships between those tables are well determined.

Transaction Management: This ensures integrity for data in a transaction through the application of the ACID properties, which further explicated represent Atomicity, Consistency, Isolation, and Durability. This technically means that the transaction will be fully executed with no variance occurring due to system failure or on account of concurrent operations that might change the data's correctness and consistency.

These mechanisms, protecting data from unauthorized access on one hand, while securing its integrity—accuracy, reliability and consistency, on the other — are therefore, very fundamental to issues of trust and conformance, with prescriptions, in several different sectors.

Advanced Topics in Data Management Distributed Databases

Distributed DBMS Concepts: Distributed Database Management Systems deal with databases spread over more than one physical location or node, which may be geographically apart. Unlike centralized systems, a DDBMS would show a single view of the data despite the distribution. Major concepts are:

Distributed Architecture: In this system, there may be several interconnected nodes running their own DBMS Software individually. Nodes cooperate to provide coherent and integrated views of a database.

Data Distribution: The distribution of data across nodes can be done through partitioning or replication. Partitioning actually divides data, and then their units are kept on different nodes. Replication, on the other hand, leads to duplication of data for better availability in terms of data and fault tolerance.

Transparency: A DDBMS should offer the facility of location transparency, such that it shields the users from having to know physically where the data is; replication transparency, where it shields the user from knowledge regarding whether or not certain data has been replicated; and partition transparency—where it shields the user from having to know how data are distributed.

Concurrency Control and Distributed Transactions: This ensures that every access is concurrent and the data is consistent through all its nodes. Views are adopted to ensure that transactions through different nodes are consistently executed. Methods in this group include the two-phase-commit (2PC) protocol and distributed locking.

Data Distribution and Replication

Partitioning: This will be the process of breaking down a database into smaller portions of partitions across nodes to make management easy. Range-based, list-based, and hash-based techniques are ways of partitioning, all of which benefit the data management and performance of the database.

Replication: Refers to the creation of multiple copies of the data at separate nodes in order to get redundancy in a way that improves fault tolerance. Replication strategies may be synchronous, where all copies are updated at once, or asynchronous, where copies can be updated at any time as the need for consistency and desire for performance allows.

NoSQL Databases

NoSQL databases are designed to work well with unstructured or semi-structured data and to scale out in order to handle large volumes of various data types. They are particularly suitable for scenarios where traditional relational databases may not perform efficiently. Some of the core features of NoSQL databases are:

Schema Flexibility: These databases keep dynamic data models that can change with time, meaning most NoSQL databases do not require a fixed schema for the stored data.

Scalability: The distribution of data into different servers or clusters to allow them to handle greater loads and volumes of data leads to a focus on this kind of scaling.

Highly Performant: Topping off in NoSQL design products is the development of databases modelled according to the use case to administer excellent performance in the retrieval of data and the manipulation of data by way of utilizing different data models and storage architectures.

Types of NoSQL Databases and Use Cases

Document-oriented Databases: Store data in flexible, hierarchical formats, like JSON or BSON. For instance, MongoDB and CouchDB are suited to applications that require flexible data structures, like content management systems and real-time analytics.

Key-Value Stores: Data is represented in terms of pairs—keys mapped to particular values. Examples include Redis and Amazon DynamoDB. Key-value stores are especially well-suited for scenarios in which quick data storage and retrieval are essential—such as caching and session management.

Column-Family Stores: They specifically organize data into columns rather than rows, which is helpful when dealing with large volumes of data and complex queries. Examples include Apache Cassandra and HBase. In providing time-series data analysis and large-scale data warehousing for analysis, they are specifically useful.

Graph databases: represent and store data using graph structures, with nodes, edges, and properties; used to model more complex relationships and interconnected data. Example products include Neo4j and Amazon Neptune. Examples of uses include social media and recommendation engines.

Big Data and DBMS

Big Data can be defined as any voluminous and complex data that poses challenges to the traditional database system in terms of storage, processing, and analysis. It involves different technologies and strategies in managing Big Data.

These include, but are not limited to: **Volume, Velocity, Variety:** The Big Data refers to huge volumes, high velocity, and variety as well.

Big Data Technologies: Tools such as Hadoop and Apache Spark are developed keeping in view the very requirements of Big Data. Hadoop offers a distributed file system and a sort of processing framework named HDFS and MapReduce, respectively. On the other hand, Spark provides in-memory processing for faster analysis of data.

Integration with DBMS: Modern databases often dovetail with Big Data technologies in order to ride on their scalability and processing strengths. Hybrid systems so developed by rejoicing the relational, NoSQL, and Big Data technologies open up full functionality for extended data management and analytics.

Data lakes and warehouses: If data lakes are specifically designed for storage at scale of raw and unstructured data, data warehouses are highly optimized—especially meant—for structured data and to hold such data that would assist complex queries. Both, therefore, are important ingredients of Big Data ecosystems for storage, management, and analytics of large datasets to unearth insights in aiding decision-making.

Now, these are truly emerging topics that are shaping the data management landscape: distributed databases, NoSQL technologies, and Big Data solutions. These items actually answer very specific needs and therefore offer remedies in dealing with very heterogeneous and complex data environments.

Future Trends in Database Management

The database management landscape has been fast-changing over the past decade because of technological developments and changing business requirements. Some important trends involved in shaping the future of a DBMS are cloud databases and integrations with some emerging technologies like AI, machine learning, and blockchain to add support for some newer types of data and workloads. Each trend has deep implications for the ways data is stored, managed, and used.

Cloud Databases

A radical move, then, to a cloud environment from traditional on-premise database systems. Cloud databases have become the lifeblood of modern data management as most organizations have moved their majority operations to the cloud.

Advantages

Scalability: Out of all the advantages, the most prominent feature cloud databases come with is their feature to scale resources on demand. Whether it is sudden traffic or long-term growth that an organization has to deal with, the database on the cloud will elastically scale to provide organizations with all the resources needed without upgrading hardware. This is especially useful for businesses whose workload fluctuates; they increase their scale during peak periods and decrease it during less busy periods for cost and performance optimization.

Cost efficiency: Cloud databases work on a pay-as-use or subscription model, such that the organization pays only for its usage. This model does not require huge up-front investments in hardware and reduces continuous maintenance costs. Moreover, sharing the cloud's infrastructure can significantly decrease costs as compared to running a dedicated in-house data center.

Accessibility and Flexibility: Cloud-based databases offer the possibility of accessing them from anywhere using an internet connection, thus aiding teleworking or team work between members spread across distinct geographic locations. Their highly flexible nature supports modern business models that strongly rely on global operations, hence making sure that data is always available to the user from any location.

Automatic Maintenance and Upgrades: The cloud providers take up the responsibility for routine database maintenance activities such as software updates, software patching, and backing up. As a result, this reduces the administration tasks that were to be done or overseen by IT personnel, and it also ensures the database is up-to-date with new features and security upgrades. Automatic updates also help to ensure a lower potential for downtime, given that they can often be applied with service still running.

High Availability and Disaster Recovery: Cloud databases are purposely architected for high availability. They usually consist of data replication and storage in more than one data center, with automated failover protocols structured to maintain operations at all times, including the cases of hardware failure or other disruptions. Disaster recovery is also made easier because, in the cloud, there are integrated backup and recovery solutions provided by cloud vendors that facilitate quick restoring of data during disaster occurrences.

Challenges

Security and Privacy: The security of the cloud is enough, and most investments are put into making sure it is secure by the providers of the cloud. However, storing data in the cloud still carries some greater risk of getting a data breach and unauthorized access. Organizations should guarantee that cloud providers operate at the level compliant with industry standards and regulations, defining, for example, General Data Protection Regulation (GDPR) or Health Insurance Portability and Accountability Act (HIPAA), to protect their sensitive information. In addition, companies should consider employing such safety measures as data encryption and multi-factor authentication.

Vendor lock-in: Vendor lock-in refers to the overreliance or dependence on a single cloud vendor. It therefore causes the hitch in switching vendors or the expensive migration of details regarding another platform. Such dependence does mean that organizational flexibility is curtailed, and that the company can be imposed upon its will, either through price hikes or adjustments in service terms. In order to mitigate this risk, some organizations use a multi cloud strategy and services from multiple providers to avoid lock-in.

Performance and Latency: Cloud databases are accessible via the network, so the high latency experienced when accessing data from remote locations degrades database performance. In this regard, organizations have to be very careful when locating data and configuring the network infrastructure to bring out the best performance. Some hybrid cloud solutions, mixing on-premises and in-cloud resources, reduce latency in many cases, thereby improving performance.

Data Sovereignty and Compliance: Under the circumstances of international transfers, it can sometimes be tough to address regulatory requirements related to data storage and processing. In this regard, organizations must ensure that the cloud provider chosen for them provides residency options in a manner that supports local laws and regulations. Issues of data sovereignty also question the appropriateness of keeping data in a country other than that from which the data originated, hence exposing it to the scrutiny of foreign governments.

DBaaS—Database as a Service

DBaaS is a service model that belongs to clouds. It provides fully managed database solutions to businesses. It reduces the complexity of managing a database, because the infrastructure, maintenance, and scaling issues are taken care of by this solution, leaving the organization to focus on the use of a database and not its management.

Definition: DBaaS is a service in the cloud in which the database infrastructure and managerial activities are provided by a third party. A consumer interacts with his database through an API or web interface, and the provider manages activities like hardware provisioning, software installation, patch application, and backups.

Benefits

Simplified Management: Through DBaaS, an organization need not worry about procuring hardware, installing a database, or maintaining it; all such tasks are handled by a service provider, so its IT team can concentrate on more value-adding activities, like data analysis and application development.

Cost-Effective: The usual model of pricing followed by DBaaS is subscription-based or pay- as-you-go, in which costs go in line with usage, completely eliminating the need for huge upfront investments. Businesses can scale their database resources according to demand and pay only for what is used. This flexibility is very useful to startups and small businesses that are very zealous in managing the budget.

Speedy Provisioning: a matter of minutes rather than days or weeks, in which case the DBaaS solution will provision a new database. The result is that an organization can easily deploy databases in just any other kind of situation without caring much. The agility supports faster cycles of development and, therefore, enables a business to be responsive quick enough depending on the change of any given situation in the market.

Scalability: The DBaaS provides automatic scalability for dealing with variated workloads. As the volume of data keeps growing or the application's needs increase, the DBaaS itself scales the resources automatically to ensure that performance remains without the need for human interference. This makes the scale of the database compatible and, hence, able to handle peak loads efficiently.

Examples

Amazon Relational Database Service RDS (AmazonRDS): Amazon RDS is a managed service for performance-based relational databases. The service provides built-in support for various database engines, including MySQL, PostgreSQL, Oracle, and SQL Server. It automatically backs up, scales, and patches itself while offering rich features, such as encryption at rest and in transit.

Google Cloud SQL: Google Cloud SQL enables fully managed, relational databases for MySQL, PostgreSQL, and SQL Server. This requires integration with automated backups, high availability, and performance tuning. Google Cloud SQL is designed to help architects build scalable and secure applications that are easy to integrate with any other service that Google Cloud offers.

Microsoft Azure SQL Database: Azure SQL Database is the relational database service that offers built-in intelligence, high availability, and elastic ability. It contains high-security features like data masking, encryption, threat detection, etc., for organizations to meet compliance requirements.

Emerging Technologies

Fledgling technologies such as AI, machine learning, and blockchain are poised to revolutionize database management, ushering in new capabilities and challenges.

The Impact of AI and Machine Learning

Automated Database Management: AI and machine learning are more and more being used to automate the different routine tasks of database management, like performance tuning, query optimization, and anomaly detection. Such technologies analyze humongous data, allowing for the identification of patterns and coming up with recommendations or even the execution of optimizations—eliminating manual intervention and increasing overall efficiency.

Predictive Analytics: Algorithms can be used to process ancient data and make future trend and behaviour forecasts. For instance, predictive analytics will support the business in forecasting customer demand, optimizing inventory levels, or identifying a security threat before actualizing. Integration of predictive analytics with the DBMS of the organizations will lead to actionable insights that result in good decision-making.

Natural Language Processing (NLP): Through this technology, the language in which the users interact with databases is the language that users understand. This way, databases can be made more accessible to non-technical users who may avail information without actually learning difficult query languages, such as SQL. if allowed to develop to a fully-fledged state, NLP would alter the dynamics of interacting with data and make extracting valuable insights from large datasets possible.

Impact of Blockchain

Data integrity and security: With blockchain facilitating a decentralized and immutable ledger, it can be applied for a number of purposes to enhance data integrity and security. In so doing, blockchain guarantees conformity, verifiability, and resistance to unauthorized changes of data through their transaction records in a tamper-proof ledger. Specifically, the solution is useful in cases wherein the requirements regarding a very high level of trust and transparency throughout the transaction process need to be guaranteed, for instance, financial transactions, supply chain management, and digital identity verification.

Smart Contracts: Smart contracts execute themselves; hence, the terms of the agreement are directly written into lines of code. Done through a blockchain network, smart contracts automatically enforce an agreement after predetermined conditions have been met. They ease many complex transactions, largely reduce the number of intermediaries, and ensure that implementation of each part of a contract is in order. Smart contracts, in the domain of database management, can automate workflows, enforce data access policies, or bind complex multi- party transactions.

Decentralized Databases: Blockchain allows for the development of a decentralized database, where data is spread out over a number of nodes rather than located at one single place. This architecture, therefore, possesses a number of benefits including better resilience against attack, greater transparency in nature, and improved privacy. On the flip side, decentralized databases come with specific challenges, such as maintenance of consensus among a number of nodes and maintaining data consistency in a distributed environment.

These emerging trends in database management thus reflect that data storage, management, and use are entering a new era. Cloud databases and DBaaS, among other emerging technologies, will set the pace toward the future in database management. They will open new avenues for scalability, efficiency, and innovation, but also open new challenges for organizations. The future of database management will look bright and promising itself, whether by way of cloud-based solutions, integration of AI and machine learning, or simply exploitation of blockchain technology.

Chapter 7

Computing Foundation

Importance of Data

Data has been one of the most significant areas of expansion in the financial services of recent times. It therefore forms the basis of major decisions and defines strategies in various fields. In finance, data includes everything from market prices, records of transactions, economic indicators, to customer behaviour. Efficiency in collecting, processing, analysing data, and putting it into its proper context is an important aspect in the decision-making process on such issues as investment strategies, risk control, regulation, and customer engagement.

Introduction to R and Python as Outstanding Programming Languages

Among financial data, R and Python emerged as two of the most prominent programming languages possessing special strengths and capabilities. It is a language built explicitly for statistical computing and graphics. It is a language and an environment built by statisticians for featuring a wide set of tools for data analysis and visualization. Because it has the vast repository of packages available, including quantmod for financial modeling and ggplot2 for data visualization, it becomes quite useful for finance sector analysts and researchers. Special features of R cater such people, whose analysis requires minute and proper statistical data handling and visualization.

On the contrary, Python is a multifaceted, general-purpose high-level programming language. The strengths that make Python such a big name includes the vast field of application in which it can be used, from data manipulation and machine learning to the development of applications, strong libraries such as pandas for data analysis, NumPy for numerical computing, and scikit-learn for machine learning. It is an extremely flexible and robust platform for finance professionals. It is an aggregator with pluggable applications, so it fits well with web applications, APIs, and big data technologies, enlarging its space in the use of building holistic financial solutions.

Combined, R and Python together become two languages that complements each other in filling the gaps when employing one versus the other for a given task of financial data analysis. The more one can distinguish between the specific applications for which each of these languages has been designed, the more the power that can be harnessed for the greater good of the financial profession.

The Role of Data Analytics in Shaping the Finance Industry: The rise of analytics has drastically altered the face of the finance world, making it achieve all the progressions and efficiencies. Some of the key influences have been:

Improved Decision-making: Data analytics allows financial experts to make confident judgments with a basis of evidence, rather than decisions based on intuition and experience only. This results in more positive outcomes for investment strategies, risk management, and resource allocation.

Improved Risk Management: By utilizing predictive analytics, financial firms can detect a number of potential risks and vulnerabilities that might be threatening their portfolios. The organizations will, therefore, be provided with ample opportunities for the prevention of such problems from happening in advance through proactive steps and will attain stability in the long run.

Fraud Detection and Prevention: Data analytics facilitates the continuous monitoring of each transaction occurring at any point of time. It detects suspicion of certain activity and redirects it for further investigation.

Advanced algorithms detect anomalies and patterns indicative of fraud while helping to protect assets and maintain trust.

Cost Efficiency: Automation of the analysis process reduces time and resources that would otherwise be used up in manual analysis, thus cutting on costs. In turn, organizations can then utilize their resources properly and focus on the best way forward in terms of strategies.

Regulatory Compliance: The financial industry is one of the most highly regulated sectors, and compliance can be realized through data analytics. Financial institutions are able to identify gaps through the analysis of data required by the regulators, hence easily making amends and corrective measures put in place.

Data is predominant in the process that leads to the financial decision-making processes. While the use of financial information of various kinds, professionals have permission to use data analytics in enhancing strategies, managing risks among others with the overall purpose of ensuring growth in the finance world.

Introduction to R

History and Development

R is a language and environment for statistical computing and graphics. It was developed around the 90s. The origins of R date back to the early 1990s, when Robert Gentleman and Ross Ihaka of the University of Auckland, New Zealand, came up with the free and open- source R language idea. R was conceived as a different language from S and started with the implementation of S features complemented by new ones.

The official release of R started in 1995, from which time till date, it has undergone lots of changes. This project, undertaken by the R Development Core Team-a dedicated effort of several statisticians and programmers who sincerely work day in and day out-is consistently being developed and improved upon. Given the large package ecosystem, great community support, and versatility to perform all sorts of complex data analysis, R has been loved by statisticians, data scientists, and researchers for many years.

The Comprehensive R Archive Network (CRAN) hosts thousands of such packages contributed by users, which help R adapt to various applications across different domains, including finance. Its open-source nature encourages collaboration and innovation, thereby making it the tool of choice for both academic research and practical applications in finance.

Features Statistical Analysis

R has been specifically developed for statistical computing and, as such, contains a vast number of built-in functions and libraries for an enormous variety of statistical techniques, including regression analysis, hypothesis testing, timeseries analysis, and multivariate statistics. It is, therefore, a preference for most disciplined financial analysts because they often have to comprehensively apply strict statistical approaches/techniques.

Graphing

R has strong data visualization capabilities using packages like ggplot2, lattice, plotly, among many others. These provide options to create publication-quality and custom visualizations in rendering financial variables and trends that help influence better decision-making.

Extensive Package Ecosystem

Besides, there are numerous packages in the R environment adapted specifically for various applications in finance. So that, there are, for example, a quant mod package for quantitative modeling of finances, Technical Trading Rules (TTR), and Performance Analytics for analyzing portfolio performance, which extends R's functionality and applicability to financial services.

Reproducibly Research

R enables reproducibility in conducted research, using facilities such as R Markdown and interfaces to version control systems. This makes it easy for a financial professional to document, analyze and share their results transparently, reproducibly-well-suited for use cases that arise within collaborative settings and regimes of compliance in finance.

Community Support

R is developed in a very vibrant way. There is a active user community that supports R on various forums, online classes, and documentation. It is for this reason continuous improvement of the language and its packages is high.

How does it integrate?

R works with other programming languages and systems, such as Python, C++, and databases. This is friendly to most of the financial experts who might have access to the best of both worlds in class information.

Applications

R finds extensive application for a wide range of uses, drawing on its strengths in both statistical capability and data visualization. Following are several key areas in which R figures importantly

Statistical Analysis and Modelling

R claims excellent statistical analysis capabilities, which render it a very important tool for financial analysts. Through an extensive array of inbuilt functions and libraries, R is able to conduct many of the standard statistical techniques needed to be performed, such as Regression

Analysis: The financial analysts can simply develop some linear or nonlinear models using R, which in turn helps to recognize the relationship between the financial variables and also predict the future trends to act upon the investments.

Hypothesis Testing: R helps in testing the hypotheses regarding financial theories or market behaviour, and with this information, analysts can better understand the statistical significance of studies.

Descriptive Statistics: Summary statistics, including those on central tendency, dispersion, and spread, are all imperative when attempting to describe financial data. Specialty functions in packages such as stats, car, and MASS further facilitate the financial professional to advance with deeper statistical modelling of data.

Portfolio Optimization

R has innumerable application on portfolio optimization used by financial professionals to design portfolios as an optimum one, able to gather maximum returns with minimum possible risk. These include the use of certain essential techniques.

Mean-Variance Optimization: R can also be used to implement Markowitz's mean-variance optimization to compute an optimal asset allocation that maximizes expected return for a given level of risk. Analysis can be done using packages such as Portfolio Analytics and quantmod.

Efficient Frontier Analysis: R can also construct the efficient frontier, which highlights a group of optimal portfolios that provide the highest expected return for a given risk level.

Rebalancing Strategies: R allows for the construction of dynamic rebalancing strategies in order to let investors maintain their desired asset allocation over time in the presence of changing market conditions.

R, through its simulation techniques and optimization algorithms, allows one to delve into different strategies a portfolio can take, expanding one's ability to make such decisions for an investor.

Time Series Analysis and Forecasting

Time series analysis is an essential tool for finance, where R offers broad scope for analysis and financial time-series forecasting:

Decompose Trend and Seasonality: R can also be utilized to decompose a time series dataset into trend, seasonality, and noise. Hence, one can learn more about the patterns hidden in financial data. Autoregressive Integrated Moving Average (ARIMA) Modeling: R can fit the ARIMA model to time series data, from which forecasts can also be generated based on past trends.

Generalized Autoregressive Conditional Heteroskedasticity (GARCH) Models: Financial markets volatility can be modelled using the facility available in R to implement Generalized Autoregressive Conditional Heteroskedasticity (GARCH) models. These models find frequent applications in finance due to the fact that asset price volatility is usually clustered

Forecasting with Exponential Smoothing: **Forecast, series,** and **zoo** are some of the mostly used **packages for time series in R** that have enabled finance professionals to make reliable forecasts and hence make data-based informed decisions.

In other words, the range of applications for R in finance has been large indeed from statistical analysis and risk management to portfolio optimization and time series prediction. With its extensive capabilities, R has become an extremely useful tool in the hands of a financial analyst. It allows deep workout conduction, conducting analysis of observations on data. As the financial domain keeps changing fast, R will continue to add value for those interested in taking data-driven approaches to their decision-making.

Benefits of Using R

R is a really powerful programming language and has many advantages which make it very well-suited in finance.

Rich Ecosystem of Statistical Packages

One of the huge advantages of R is its rich ecosystem of statistical packages that extend the core analytical functionalities for performing a wide range of statistical tasks. For financial analysis and modeling, there are several specialized packages like quantmod, Technical Trading Rules (TTR) forecast etc.

Excellent Data Visualization Capabilities

R is also famous for its core competence in data visualization, which is the most vital element in showcasing insight and trend in finance.

R, all its sophistication, and use of visualization in the presentation of data, allows an analyst or decision-maker intuitively to perceive complex financial insights.

Strong Community Support and Resources

Another reason for R's popularity is its dynamic, growing community that extends its functionality.

In other words, R offers a lot of benefits over financial applications because of large statistical packages and better data visualization, along with its strong community support. These provide strengths that make R an indispensable tool for any financial analyst interested in sophisticated analysis, efficient data visualization, and effective communication of insights.

Overview of Python History and Evolution

Python is a high-level language. It was developed by Guido van Rossum and released in 1991. Van Rossum worked on a language that implemented code readability and simplicity so that it could be easy for a novice programmer yet powerful for advanced programmers. Regarding its design philosophy,

Python puts emphasis on clarity with the least number of lines compared to other languages when the same code will have to be written. But, of course, Python has changed dramatically with time. The 2000 release, Python 2.0, possessed a huge number of such features that were symbolic to the language: list comprehensions and a garbage collection system, for example. Actually, however, it was the 2008 release of Python 3.0 that marked the most dramatic step towards improvement. This version corrected intrinsic flaws in the original version of Python 2 and significantly enhanced the functions working within the language.

It was during this time that Python 3 was released with the intention of fixing design flaws and syntax. It introduced many backward-incompatible changes, such as modifying how print functionality worked, making integer division behave differently, and it initially defaulted to Unicode for strings, so existing Python 2 codebases needed to be modified so that they would run under Python 3.

As a result, the transition slowly occurred, putting pressure on many developers and organizations to change the code, test for compatibility, and coach the staff on new features. Consequently, it took an extremely long time before Python 2 and Python 3 could peacefully coexist, adding to a large amount of confusion, mostly among beginners. The transition also entailed hundreds of libraries and frameworks that were updated with new improvements, at considerable expense in terms of time and labour, from the development community. It was essentially due to such crucial enhancements in Python 3 that the issues of backward compatibility and legacy code were vastly impacting the Python community for years. It is one of the popular languages nowadays, because it has applications in wide domains, including web developments, data analysis, artificial intelligence, and finance. Large libraries and frameworks, along with strong community support, are the basis for growth and adoption in financial markets.

Key Features and Strengths

There are several key features and strengths of Python that have made it highly apt for financial applications:

Ease of Learning and Use

The Python syntax is clean and pretty simple to learn and use by a novice. This availability will permit financial professionals with not very rich programming backgrounds to learn the language in no time and put it to work for various types of analyses.

Extensive Libraries and Frameworks

Python has an impressive ecosystem of libraries and frameworks surrounding data analysis and financial modeling. Some of the popular libraries in this regard include: Pandas manipulate and analyze data, perform time series data, and handle big datasets. NumPy introduces numerical computation and perform mathematical functions on arrays and matrices.

SciPy introduces advanced mathematics and scientific functions. Matplotlib and Seaborn create graphs, plots, and charts with data.

Scikit-learn Machine learning; Python modules for data mining and predictive modeling are provided.

Integrations

Python is easily integrated with other programming languages like C, C++, and R, databases like SQL, and web services. That makes it a very versatile tool that enables financial analysts to use an extraordinary number of different instruments and technologies in their workflows. **Full Support for Object-Oriented Programming:**

Python enables object-oriented programming for its users. In the case of Python, object-oriented programming permits the user to create modular and reusable code. This is very helpful in developing sophisticated financial models and systems and helps in keeping the code organized and maintainable.

Community and Resources

Python is developed by an active, vibrant community that contributes to its features and provides extensive support. The volumes of online forums, tutorials, and documentation contribute in making access to help and other resources develop skills for the user.

Cross-Platform Compatibility

Python is cross-operable, that means one can use it easily on any operating system, like Windows, macOS, or Linux. It is for this reason, because of the flexibility associated with it, financial analysts can work with Python in a various set of environments and collaboration across different systems.

General, Python is a multi-capable, dynamic and user-friendly language with rich history and high penetrative ability in the financial world. Due to its ease of use, abundant libraries, and integrative capabilities, it should be the go-to choose for any financial analyst that wants to do fancy analytics, build predictive models, or simply automate a workflow with ease.

Uses of Python

Combined with the flexibility of Python, coupled with robust libraries, which has cemented the language as dominant in financial services, here are some important uses of Python in finance.

Data Manipulation and Analysis

Python is extremely efficient for dealing and analyzing data, equipped with very powerful tools and libraries suited for manipulation and analytical tasks on data.

Pandas: This is a **library which has mainly been developed for data manipulation and analysis**, for easy handling of structured data using structures such as DataFrames. It also provides facilities for data cleaning, data filtering, aggregating, and merging datasets-very essential while working with large financial datasets.

NumPy: This is one of the most **important libraries for Python and deals with all types of numerical computing**. It supports multi-dimensional arrays, as well as high-level mathematical functions to work on these arrays. Financial analysts use NumPy in accomplishing vectorized operations, which allows better computation while working on big data.

Data Retrieval: Python can use financial APIs such as Alpha Vantage and Yahoo Finance to extract both real-time and historical financial data. This enables an analyst to pull market data into the workflow for further processing.

Machine Learning and Predictive Modeling

As practice continues, the use of Python is increasing immensely in machine learning and predictive modeling within finance, with various libraries that reduce the burden of complex Algorithm implementation.

Scikit-learn: This library provides an advanced set of machine learning algorithms for classification, regression, clustering, and dimensionality reduction. Financial people construct predictive models using Scikit-learn to predict credit scores, assess risk, and forecast the prices that will be passed on to the stock.

TensorFlow and Keras: These libraries are useful in higher-order machine learning tasks such as deep learning. Financial analysts make use of such frameworks in order to build and train neural networks on complex predictive modeling, such as the forecasting of market trends or identification of trading patterns.

Feature Engineering: The libraries of Python make feature engineering very efficient; this helps analysts create meaningful variables from raw data, hence improving the accuracy of their models.

Algorithmic Trading and Automation

Python plays an important role in algorithmic trading and automation, allowing traders to actually design a strategy they want to be implemented and executed in a programmatic manner.

Strategy Back testing: Back testing enables the analyst to try out a trading strategy on historical data to establish whether the strategy is viable to the extent of being profitable enough for them to consider using in a live market. The Back trader and Zipline libraries make it even easier to develop and test trading algorithms.

Trading Automation: Python basically automates trading by order execution and portfolio management. Traders create an automated trading system using APIs provided by various brokerage platforms like Interactive Brokers and Alpaca. The system responds in real-time to changes in market conditions.

Data Processing and Analysis: Python automates data collection and its preprocessing tasks so that the trader gets the most updated information for making the decisions.

Data Visualization:

Data visualization is very much necessary to bring out the financial insight. Python has developed some of the most powerful libraries in building informative and interactive visualizations. A few of them are: Matplotlib, Seaborn, Plotly.

Python has applications in finance from mere data manipulation and analysis to machine learning, algorithmic trading, and financial data visualization. With the broad range of libraries and frameworks, Python empowers financial professionals to perform advanced analysis, create predictive models and automate workflows in a very effective way.

R vs Python: Comparative Analysis

It is necessary to investigate both R and Python in the sphere of their strong and weak points while selecting which programming language is better for financial uses. Each of the languages has its own attributes suitable for different needs in statistical analysis, data visualization, and the requirements of the projects.

Strengths and Weaknesses

Statistical Analysis and Data Visualization R

Strengths

R is moulded toward statistical analysis and data visualization. It uses a broad range of statistical functions and packages, making it the favourite tool of many statisticians and data scientists.

Meanwhile, it is possible to conduct advanced visualization and manipulation through libraries such as ggplot2, dplyr, and tidyverse, whereby it has become easy for users to make complex visualizations.

Weaknesses

R consumes more time than Python when one has huge data. The syntax used in R can be irresistible for the user starting out in statistical programming.

Python

Strengths

Python is generally a multifunctional language with statistics as one of its applications, making it likely to serve for other purposes outside the strict purview of statistics—for instance, data manipulation, web development, and machine learning. Concerning data analysis and visualization, support comes through libraries like Pandas and Matplotlib, respectively, although they are not as specialized as those by R.

It is more syntactically intuitive, hence more accessible to new users. Adoption and deployment are easier.

Weaknesses

For Python, performs anything that R can with respect to statistical analysis - sometimes it

Takes more work, especially for higher-end statistical functionality. Visualization libraries might not be quite as robust, or accessible, as explicit R visualizations for complex statistical graphics.

Ease of Use and Learning Curve R

Strengths

R is designed for statisticians and data scientists with built-in functions making statistical analysis easier. When the initial learning curve is over, analysis can be very quick and easy to implement.

Weaknesses

R is not friendly to new users who have no experience in statistics or programming. The syntax and structure of this programming language will seem quite awkward at first.

Python

Strengths

Python syntax is clear and readable and, therefore, can be used by a beginner and professional, having an experience in other fields. This ease makes its user concentrate on their analysis but not the details of the programming language.

Weakness

The flexible nature of Python sometimes attributes to confusion, especially in beginners, on what libraries to apply to what, and this may actually slow down the learning process.

Community Support and Documentation R

Strengths

R has a vibrant community that is focused on statisticians and data scientists, with a lot of documentation, forums, and resources available. A lot of effort is put into developing packages for the statistical needs by the community, and they are under continuous improvement and support.

Weaknesses

The R community, in general, is relatively smaller compared to Python and so maybe not so good for general programming questions or wide applications beyond statisticians and data scientists.

Python Strengths

Python supports a very active community that ranges from finance to web development and data science, so there are definitely rich resources available, including tutorials, documentation, and forums to help users.

Weaknesses

Python is so well documented that sometimes it can be a bit overwhelming for the user seeking simple, direct answers to specific financial application queries.

Challenges in Using R

Even though R provides considerable simplification for the purpose of statistical analysis and data visualization, it does have associated   challenges.

Steeper Learning Curve for Beginners

R is tailored for some specific purposes in statistical computing, so it can be quite complex for a person who has a poor statistical or programming background. For example, learners find its syntax and the data structures associated with it, like data frames and lists, confusing. This does make the learning curve steep and prohibitive in quickly onboarding projects for people used to more general programming languages.

Limited Capabilities for Developing Standalone Applications

R is more of a statistical programming language than a tool for building stand-alone applications or software to be used at a production level. Although packages like Shiny allow for the deployment of web applications meant for the visualization and interactive analysis of data, most of these applications are not very robust or scalable when considered for use in large projects. The second aspect might be limiting for financial institutions that either intend to extend the use of R-based solutions more broadly into their operations or incorporate them into current technology stacks.

Challenges of Using Python

Python is indeed a multi-purpose and widely applicable language as a programming tool however, Python also has its challenges in the context of financial applications.

Less Specialized for Certain Statistical Tasks Compared to R

Although Python has powerful libraries for data analysis, such as Pandas and NumPy, it is not very specialized when it comes to very advanced statistical analysis and modeling in comparison to R. Hence, often users have to use additional libraries or tools to manage some specific tasks in statistics, which makes the working process more complicated and takes more time when developing certain models.

Complexity in the Management of Dependencies for Large Projects

Large projects, with many complex interactions between different Python libraries, can make managing library dependencies very complex. With so many libraries depending on other libraries each possibly at different versions, there is a good chance of running into compatibility issues. This becomes even more of an issue in finance, where accuracy and reliability are crucial. To solve this, developers need to spend much time managing environments with tools like virtualenv or conda.

Both R and Python serve their respective challenges and limitations, which users should consider when making this decision for finance applications. The steeper learning curve and relatively lower capacity for developing applications in R have been able to complicate things for using such tools—especially for beginners or who needs to build strong applications. On the other hand, Python is general, so getting into some of the specialized statistical tasks may require some workarounds, and with larger projects, handling dependencies can become painful. Understanding these challenges helps a financial professional make an informed decision on the choice of language depending on particular project needs and team skills. **Emerging Trends**

For the world of evolving finance, several trends may be expected which would shape the future of programming languages R and Python. These are due to advances in technology, alterations of consumer behavioural mindsets, and new emerging challenges in financial markets.

Rise of AI and ML: AI and, ML have found a way to enhance functionality for the customer as risk management, fraud detection, customer support, and investment strategy. Big data analytics help financial institutions to uncover such dynamics that would be excessively difficult to reach prior and decisively act based on findings.

R and Python for prediction models and algo trading: While R and Python both provide immense support for the development of predictive models that can be driven with AI and ML algorithms, R's comprehensive statistical packages make it a popular choice for building complex statistical models. Python's versatility and libraries TensorFlow, scikit-learn-facilitate implementation related to machine learning. Both languages can be used in developing automated trading strategies to take immediate leads from market signals, hence improving the efficiency and profitability of the trading exercise.

Growth of Data-Driven Decision-Making

The Trend towards Personalization of Financial Services Driven by Data Analytics: The financial arena is going toward personalization in a big way. This is tailored to the individual customer profile of products and recommendations. These are based on insights from the data captured, hence enabling the institutions to understand the behaviour and preference of customers better. Personalized offerings shall improve satisfaction and loyalty gained from a more satisfied customer base.

Linked to Big Data Technologies

Big data technologies are increasingly being employed within the financial industry to handle rising volumes, velocity, and variety. Big data platforms like Apache Spark and Hadoop allow organizations to process and analyze large volumes of financial data. Therein lies much of its importance, especially for risk analysis, meeting regulatory requirements, and even real-time analytics.

The future of finance will be shaped by the three trends of intensifying use of AI and machine learning, increased data-driven decision-making, and integration of technologies that power big data. R and Python are going to play some significant roles in the advances of this dimension, from data analytics to predictive modeling of the financial institutions. The financial sector is changing very fast, and practitioners in this domain will be most heavily using these two language skills to maximize their potentials for effectively solving complicated problems and streamlining the processes of decisions.

In a world of continuous growth and change, R and Python are two well-known programming languages with their own particular advantages in finance for the execution of data analyses, modeling and decision-making.

Future Trends in R and Python

Both R and Python are on a very good trajectory for a tremendous change and evolution in the future of data science and analytics, leading to technological advancement and new users' needs.

R

R is becoming more powerful with integration support for other programming languages such as Python, C++, etc. to allow the best capability of every programming language available for use in different kinds of analytical tasks by the data scientist. This is complemented by the emerging Tidyverse, a suite of R packages that have the objective of making data manipulation and visualization flow as smoothly and elegantly as possible, developed as an exemplary instance of a tidy data philosophy. As R continues to evolve, "the emphasis on dynamic report generation through tools like R Markdown will provide the user with an easy-to-use means of bringing code, narrative and visualizations together to elucidate the findings drawn from the data.".

Further, R is specializing in its capabilities in machine learning with packages like caret, mlr, and tidymodels that help it try toward a more user-friendly way of building and evaluating models. Improved capabilities for data visualization-primarily through ggplot2-will be enhanced, such that users can create really complex visualizations of their data and stories. This will make R even more attractive to non-programmers, as the wide availability of user- friendly interfaces will democratize access to data science. Cloud computing will also help to scale up and collaborate in data analysis, which R will naturally smoothen by integrating it with cloud-based platforms.

Python

On the other hand, simplicity will keep on driving Python's stronghold in data science and artificial intelligence, with significant momentum in action, pushing forward with robust ecosystems of libraries like NumPy, Pandas, TensorFlow, and PyTorch. Growth in the machine learning frameworks will simply further enlarge the domain of applications of deep learning based on Python but improve usability and performance along the way. Data science is next going to depend on Jupyter Notebooks where it will be used as an interactive tool for the purpose of data exploration and relating finding.

Automation would be next in the list of focuses for the data science group, and Python is going to become the preferred programming language as it is being widely used just to write scripts for the automation of repetitive procedures concerning data manipulation hence increasing the efficiency of workflows. In addition, the development of data visualization libraries such as Matplotlib, Seaborn, and Plotly will enable richer and more interactive visual storytelling that will be necessary for stakeholder communication with complex data insights. More compatibility of Python with large-scale big data technologies, like Apache Spark and Dask, will allow data scientists to deal with bigger datasets and process them remotely.

Conclusion

The future landscape of data science will definitely be fashioned by R and Python because they continue to evolve with improvements that serve user needs, enhance capabilities, and foster ethical practices in data analytics.

Chapter 8

Tools and Techniques in Financial Analytics

To analyse, understand, and make well-informed decisions based on financial data, financial analytics tools and methodologies are crucial. They support businesses in monitoring performance, evaluating risks, and spotting lucrative prospects. These methods and tools are essential for the following reasons:

1. Data Collection and Processing

- **Need**: Large volumes of financial data need to be gathered and processed efficiently.

- **Tools/Techniques**: SQL databases, data scraping, and ETL (Extract, Transform, Load) tools are widely used to gather and prepare data for analysis.

2. Statistical Analysis and Modeling

- **Need**: Understanding trends, patterns, and relationships within financial data for predicting future performance.

- **Tools/Techniques**: Statistical software like R, SAS, and Python libraries (NumPy, Pandas) are used for regression analysis, hypothesis testing, and time-series analysis.

3. Financial Forecasting and Predictive Analytics

- **Need**: Estimating future values like revenue, expenses, or stock prices to aid in decision-making.

- **Tools/Techniques**: Techniques include time-series forecasting, machine learning models (like ARIMA, neural networks), and financial modeling with tools like Excel, Python, and dedicated platforms such as MATLAB.

4. Risk Management

- **Need**: Identifying and mitigating financial risks to protect against potential losses.

- **Tools/Techniques**: Value at Risk (VaR), Monte Carlo simulation, and credit risk models. Tools include risk management software like Palisade's @RISK, MATLAB, and specialized financial analytics platforms.

5. Data Visualization

- **Need**: Presenting financial data and analysis in a clear, easily interpretable way for stakeholders.

- **Tools/Techniques**: Visualization tools like Tableau, Power BI, and Python's Matplotlib and Seaborn libraries to create charts, dashboards, and reports.

6. Portfolio and Asset Management

- **Need**: Optimizing asset allocation to maximize returns while minimizing risk.

- **Tools/Techniques**: Portfolio optimization techniques such as the Markowitz model, CAPM, and Python's PyPortfolioOpt, as well as platforms like Bloomberg Terminal and Morningstar.

7. Big Data and Real-Time Analysis

- **Need**: Handling high-frequency trading data and large datasets for real-time decision- making.

- **Tools/Techniques**: Big data tools like Apache Spark, Hadoop, and cloud computing services (AWS, Azure) for processing large data sets and deriving insights in real-time.

These tools and techniques in financial analytics not only provide better insights but also help streamline decision-making, risk assessment, and performance evaluation. The following tools are widely used in finance.

1. Tableau:

   This robust data visualisation application enables users to produce dynamic, eye-catching dashboards and reports. It is appropriate for financial research and reporting since it can link to multiple data sources, such as databases, spreadsheets, and cloud services.

2. Microsoft Power BI:

   Users may see and analyse data from many sources with Microsoft's business analytics application, Power BI. Because of its interactive dashboards, real-time analytics, and sophisticated data modelling features, it may be used for forecasting, decision-making, and financial reporting.

3. QlikView/Qlik Sense:

   These business intelligence and data visualisation tools enable users to explore and analyse data in order to find patterns and come to well-informed conclusions. They are appropriate for financial analysis and reporting because they provide strong data visualisation capabilities and support for data integration.

4. SAS Business Analytics:

   SAS provides a range of business analytics tools that let users carry out sophisticated analytics, such as forecasting, optimisation, and predictive modelling. Sophisticated financial analytics jobs can benefit from its solutions for risk management, fraud detection, and financial planning.

5.   IBM Cognos Analytics:

IBM offers data exploration, dashboards, reporting, and other business intelligence functionalities through its Cognos Analytics platform. Predictive modelling is among the sophisticated analytics features it provides and scenario planning, which qualifies it for use in performance management and financial analysis.

6.   Alteryx:

This data analytics tool lets users prepare, combine, and examine data from many sources. It is appropriate for financial analytics and data-driven decision-making since it provides sophisticated analytics features like predictive modelling, geographical analysis, and machine learning.

7.   R and Python:

Frequently utilized for statistical analysis, data visualization, and machine learning, R and Python are open-source programming languages. They are well-liked by data scientists and financial analysts since they provide a large selection of libraries and packages made especially for financial analytics.

8.   Bloomberg Terminal:

Professionals in the finance business frequently utilise Bloomberg Terminal, a platform for financial data and analytics. It gives users access to the current market. It is essential for financial analysis, trading, and investment management since it contains data, news, research, and analytical tools.

These are but a handful of the many financial analytics solutions on the market. The organization's unique requirements, the analysis's complexity, and the users' skill level all play a role in the tool selection.

Tableau usage in Financial Analysis

Tableau is a popular application for data visualisation in the financial analytics industry because of its robust features, user-friendliness, and capacity to produce dynamic, eye-catching dashboards. Tableau is frequently used in the following financial analytics use cases:

1. Financial Reporting:

    With Tableau, analysts of finance may design dynamic dashboards and reports that show financial data, including cash flow, balance sheet, income, and ratios. Users can examine trends, patterns, and outliers in the data by drilling down into individual details.

2. Performance Analysis:

    Investment portfolios, mutual funds, and individual securities can all be subject to performance analyses by financial analysts using Tableau. In order to compare performance measures like returns, volatility, Sharpe ratio, and benchmark comparisons across time, they can build dashboards.

3. Risk Management:

    Market, credit, and operational risks are just a few of the hazards that Tableau is used to visualise and analyse in risk management. To keep track of risk exposures, run stress tests, and examine how risk factors affect financial performance, analysts can build dashboards.

4. Budgeting and Forecasting:

    Tableau is used to analyse previous financial data, spot trends, and project figures for next periods in budgeting and forecasting procedures. To compare actual performance to budgeted targets and pinpoint deviations for each given goal, users can develop dynamic dashboards.

5.   Financial Planning and Analysis (FP&A):

To track financial metrics, analyse key performance indicators (KPIs), and assist in decision- making, Tableau is utilised in FP&A procedures. Dashboards that show revenue projections, spending patterns, profitability analyses, and scenario planning can be made by analysts.

6.   Client Analytics:

In the financial services sector, Tableau is used to analyse client data and behaviour. To enhance marketing strategies and boost customer retention, analysts can build dashboards that provide customer demographics, segmentation, acquisition patterns, churn analysis, and lifetime value analysis.

7.   Compliance and Regulatory Reporting:

Basel III, the Dodd-Frank Act, and Anti-Money Laundering (AML) rules are just a few of the regulations that Tableau is used to monitor and manage through compliance dashboards and reports.

8.   Fraud Detection and Prevention:

Transaction data may be visualised and analysed using Tableau, which can also be used to spot trends and abnormalities that can point to fraud. Dashboards can be made by analysts to keep an eye on questionable transactions, look into alerts, and reduce the chance of fraud.

In general, Tableau is a flexible tool that helps financial analysts to efficiently explore, analyse, and visualise financial data, which promotes better financial analytics performance, better insights, and better decision-making.

Usage of Microsoft Power BI in financial analytics

Because of its many features, easy interface with Excel and other Microsoft products, and capacity to build dynamic and eye-catching dashboards,

Microsoft Power BI is extensively utilised in the financial analytics space. Here are some typical financial analytics use cases for

Power BI:

1. Financial Reporting:

    Income statements, balance sheets, cash flow statements, and financial ratios may all be visually represented in interactive reports and dashboards that financial analysts can develop using Power BI. Users are able to examine trends, patterns, and outliers in the data by drilling down into individual details.

2. Budgeting and Forecasting:

    To evaluate past financial data, spot trends, and project numbers for upcoming times, budgeting and forecasting procedures employ Power BI.

    In order to do variance analysis, evaluate actual performance versus budgeted targets, and aid in decision-making, users can develop dynamic dashboards.

3. Performance Analysis:

    Investment portfolios, mutual funds, or individual securities can all have their performance examined using Power BI. To evaluate performance data like returns, volatility, Sharpe ratio, and benchmark comparisons across time, financial analysts can build dashboards.

4. Risk Management:

    Market risk, credit risk, and operational risk are just a few of the hazards that can be visualised and analysed using Power BI. To keep track of risk exposures, perform stress tests, and examine how risk factors affect financial performance, analysts can build dashboards.

5. Financial Planning and Analysis (FP&A):

    Key performance indicators (KPIs) are analysed, financial data is tracked, and FP&A procedures use Power BI.

6. Client Analytics:

    In the financial services sector, Power BI is utilised to examine client information and behaviour. To enhance marketing strategies and boost customer retention, analysts can build dashboards that provide customer demographics, segmentation, acquisition patterns, churn analysis, and lifetime value analysis.

7. Compliance and Regulatory Reporting:

    Basel III, the Dodd-Frank Act, and anti-money laundering (AML) rules are just a few of the regulations that may be tracked and compliance needs to be ensured by using Power BI to generate compliance dashboards and reports.

8. Fraud Detection and Prevention:

    Transaction data is visualised and analysed using Power BI, which also helps to spot trends and abnormalities that may point to fraudulent activity. Dashboards can be made by analysts to keep an eye on questionable transactions, look into alerts, and reduce the chance of fraud.

    In general, Power BI is a flexible tool that helps financial analysts to efficiently explore, analyse, and visualise financial data, which promotes superior financial analytics performance, insights, and decision-making.

Usage of QlikView/Qlik Sense in financial analytics

Financial analytics makes extensive use of the robust business intelligence and data visualisation tools QlikView and Qlik Sense. In the financial sector, QlikView and Qlik Sense are frequently used in the following scenarios:

1. Financial Reporting:

   Financial analysts can generate interactive reports and dashboards using QlikView/Qlik Sense to visualise financial data, including cash flow statements, balance sheets, income statements, and financial ratios. Users can examine trends, compare performance over various time periods or business units, and drill down into precise details.

2. Budgeting and Forecasting:

   To analyse past financial data, spot trends, and project numbers for next periods, budgeting and forecasting procedures employ QlikView/Qlik Sense. To enhance decision-making, users can design dynamic dashboards that track actual performance versus budgeted targets and do deviation analysis.

3. Performance Analysis:

   Investment portfolios, mutual funds, or individual securities can all be subject to performance analyses using QlikView/Qlik Sense. To evaluate performance data like returns, volatility, Sharpe ratio, and benchmark comparisons across time, financial analysts can build dashboards.

4. Risk Management:

   Market risk, credit risk, and operational risk are just a few of the hazards that may be visualised and analysed with QlikView/Qlik Sense. To keep track of risk exposures, perform stress tests, and examine how risk factors affect financial performance, analysts can build dashboards.

5. Financial Planning and Analysis (FP&A):

   To track financial metrics, analyse key performance indicators (KPIs), and assist in decision-making, FP&A processes make use of

QlikView/Qlik Sense. Dashboards that show revenue projections, spending patterns, profitability analyses, and scenario analysis can be made by analysts.

6.   Client Analytics:

The financial services sector uses QlikView/Qlik Sense to analyse client data and behaviour. To enhance marketing strategies and boost customer retention, analysts can build dashboards that provide customer demographics, segmentation, acquisition patterns, churn analysis, and lifetime value analysis.

7.   Compliance and Regulatory Reporting:

Basel III, the Dodd-Frank Act, and Anti-Money Laundering (AML) rules are just a few of the regulations that can be monitored and complied with with the use of QlikView/Qlik Sense compliance dashboards and reports.

8.   Fraud Detection and Prevention:

Transaction data is visualised and analysed using QlikView/Qlik Sense, which also helps to spot abnormalities and patterns that point to possible fraudulent activity. Dashboards can be made by analysts to keep an eye on questionable transactions, look into alerts, and reduce the chance of fraud.

In general, QlikView and Qlik Sense are flexible tools that let financial analysts successfully explore, analyse, and visualise financial data. This results in better financial analytics performance, greater insights, and better decision-making.

Usage of SAS Business Analytics in financial analytics

Financial analytics with SAS Business Analytics

The finance industry makes extensive use of SAS Business Analytics, a full suite of analytics tools provided by SAS Institute, for a variety of applications. The following are a few typical financial use cases for SAS Business Analytics:

1. Risk management:

    To evaluate and reduce the range of risks that financial institutions encounter, SAS Business Analytics is widely utilised in risk management. Credit, market, liquidity, operational, and compliance risks are all included in this. SAS offers sophisticated analytics functionalities to assess the possible consequences of risk occurrences by modelling risk factors, computing risk metrics, conducting scenario analysis, and stress testing.

2. Fraud Detection and Prevention:

    To identify and stop fraudulent activity in financial transactions, SAS Business Analytics is used. For the purpose of identifying suspicious patterns, odd behaviours, and fraudulent transactions, SAS provides strong fraud detection models, anomaly detection algorithms, and predictive analytics tools. In order to reduce financial losses, financial institutions utilise SAS to track transactions in real-time, look into alarms, and put fraud protection measures in place.

3. Customer analytics:

    SAS Business Analytics is used to examine consumer behaviour and data in order to understand their needs, preferences, and actions. In order to improve customer satisfaction and loyalty, financial institutions use SAS to segment their client base based on demographics, behaviours, and transactional patterns. They then use this data to create tailored marketing campaigns, offers, and customer retention initiatives.

4. Credit Risk Assessment:

    To determine borrowers' creditworthiness and the probability of default, credit risk assessment uses SAS Business Analytics. Using borrower data, credit history, financial ratios, and macroeconomic factors, SAS offers sophisticated credit scoring models, statistical algorithms, and machine learning techniques to help lenders make well-informed decisions and efficiently manage credit risk.

5. Financial Planning and Forecasting:

    To analyse past financial data, spot trends, and project for upcoming periods, financial planning and forecasting use SAS Business Analytics. In order to maximise resource allocation, enhance decision-making, and meet financial objectives, financial institutions utilise SAS to create forecasting models, budgeting tools, and scenario planning capabilities.

6. Performance Measurement:

    Portfolios, investment strategies, and financial products are all subject to performance evaluation and measurement through the use of SAS Business Analytics. Financial institutions may analyse returns, risk-adjusted returns, attribution analysis, and benchmark comparisons with the help of SAS's extensive performance measurement and attribution capabilities. This helps them evaluate investment performance, track portfolio dynamics, and make the best possible investment decisions.

7. Regulatory Compliance and Reporting:

    SAS Business Analytics is utilised in the banking industry to guarantee adherence to reporting standards and regulatory obligations. SAS provides data governance frameworks, regulatory reporting solutions, and compliance analytics capabilities to assist financial institutions in adhering to laws like Basel III, the

Dodd-Frank Act, Know Your Customer (KYC) standards, and Anti-Money Laundering (AML) rules.

All things considered, SAS Business Analytics offers financial institutions a full range of tools and capacities that they can use to better manage risk, make better decisions, and propel business performance in the fast-paced, heavily regulated finance sector. These tools and capabilities include predictive modelling, advanced analytics, and data-driven insights.

IBM Cognos Analytics usage in financial analytics

Financial analytics with IBM Cognos Analytics is a business intelligence and performance management platform that offers a number of analytics, dashboarding, reporting, and data visualization tools. IBM Cognos Analytics is widely utilized for a number of reasons in the financial sector, including:

1. Financial Reporting and Analysis:

    Financial experts can generate interactive reports and dashboards using IBM Cognos Analytics to examine financial data, including cash flow statements, balance sheets, income statements, and financial ratios. To aid in financial planning and decision-making, users can explore in- depth information, visualise patterns, and learn more about key performance indicators (KPIs).

2. Budgeting and Forecasting:

    To analyse past financial data, spot trends, and project numbers for next periods, budgeting and forecasting procedures employ IBM Cognos Analytics. Financial analysts can optimise resource allocation, enhance decision-making, and accomplish financial objectives by developing dynamic budgeting models, scenario planning tools, and rolling forecasts.

3. Performance Management:

   Financial organisations can track and measure performance in a number of areas, such as customers, channels, products, and geographical areas, with the help of IBM Cognos Analytics. To find areas for improvement and promote operational efficiency, users can monitor key performance indicators (KPIs), perform performance variance analysis, and compare actual performance against targets.

4. Risk Management:

   Identifying, evaluating, and reducing risks in a variety of contexts, such as credit, market, liquidity, and operational risk, are all possible with IBM Cognos Analytics. Financial organisations optimise risk-adjusted returns and assure regulatory compliance by using IBM Cognos Analytics to create risk dashboards, conduct stress tests, and analyse risk exposures.

5. Customer Analytics:

   To learn more about the preferences, needs, and behaviours of customers, IBM Cognos Analytics is used to analyse customer data and behaviour. To increase customer satisfaction, retention, and loyalty, financial institutions utilise IBM Cognos Analytics to segment their client base, evaluate customer lifetime value, and create tailored marketing campaigns and offers.

6. Regulatory Compliance and Reporting:

   Basel III, the Dodd-Frank Act, Anti-Money Laundering (AML) laws, and Know Your Customer (KYC) requirements are just a few of the regulations that financial institutions must abide by. IBM Cognos Analytics offers tools for regulatory compliance and reporting. In addition to making sure that regulations are followed, users can also create regulatory reports and track compliance data.

7. Predictive Analytics:

Financial professionals may foresee future trends, predict customer behaviour, and discover new risks and opportunities by utilising IBM Cognos Analytics' advanced analytics capabilities, which include predictive modelling, machine learning, and statistical analysis. Predictive analytics can be used by users to optimise corporate operations, make data-driven decisions, and obtain a competitive edge in the marketplace. All things considered, IBM Cognos Analytics offers a full range of tools and capabilities that let financial organisations take advantage of data-driven insights, cutting-edge analytical methods, and performance management skills to enhance decision-making, spur corporate expansion, and accomplish strategic goals in the fast-paced, heavily regulated financial sector.

Alteryx's application in financial analytics:

Usage of Alteryx in financial analytics:

Alteryx is a powerful data analytics platform that is widely used in various industries, including finance. In the realm of financial analytics, Alteryx can be applied in several ways:

1. Data Preparation and Cleaning:

Financial data is frequently disorganized or lacking from multiple sources. Analysts can clean, consolidate, and standardize financial data for additional analysis by using Alteryx's data preparation, transformation, and cleansing capabilities.

2. Data Integration:

Spreadsheets, databases, and cloud services are just a few of the sources of data that users may combine with Alteryx. This feature is useful in financial analytics for combining data from many financial systems and sources, including market data providers, trading platforms, and accounting software.

3. Predictive Analytics:

    Financial parameters like sales, revenue, expenses, and stock prices can be forecasted with the use of Alteryx's predictive analytics tools. Alteryx's machine learning algorithms allow analysts to create predictive models that may be used to spot trends, patterns, and outliers.

4. Risk Management:

    Alteryx is used by financial organisations for fraud detection, credit risk assessment, and compliance reporting. The predictive modelling and data blending capabilities of Alteryx can assist organisations in identifying possible hazards and taking proactive steps to reduce them.

5. Portfolio Analysis:

    Alteryx is useful for risk profiling, asset allocation, and performance attribution in investment portfolio analysis. Alteryx is a tool that analysts can use to compile portfolio data, determine key performance indicators (KPIs), and provide reports to stakeholders.

6. Financial Reporting:

    Cash flow statements, balance sheets, and income statements are just a few of the financial reports that Alteryx can automate. Organisations may assure accuracy and consistency in their financial reporting by streamlining the reporting process and automating data processing through connections to financial systems.

7. Customer Segmentation and Analysis:

    Targeting particular customer segments with customised financial products and services requires the use of customer segmentation, which is essential in the finance sector. Organisations may personalise their services and increase customer satisfaction and retention by using Alteryx to segment clients based on their financial behaviour, demographics, and preferences.

8. Compliance and Regulatory Reporting:

    Alteryx can help automate compliance procedures and produce regulatory reports. Financial institutions must adhere to a number of regulatory regulations. Organisations can guarantee regulatory compliance and lower the risk of fines or penalties by implementing preset business rules and integrating data from various sources.

    All things considered, Alteryx offers a scalable and adaptable financial analytics platform that helps businesses to learn from their financial data, make wise decisions,

Usage of R and Python in financial analytics

Because of their adaptability, vast libraries, and strong statistical skills, R and Python are two of the most widely used computer languages in financial analytics. The following describes how financial analytics often uses each language:

R in Financial Analytics:

1. Statistical Analysis: R is well-known for its extensive statistical powers, which make it perfect for a wide range of financial data analyses, including regression analysis, time series analysis, hypothesis testing, and descriptive statistics.

2. Visualisation: To visualise financial trends, patterns, and insights, analysts can construct interactive, publication-quality charts, graphs, and dashboards using R's robust data visualisation tools, such as ggplot2 and plotly.

3. Financial Modelling: To create intricate financial models, such as option pricing models, portfolio optimisation models, risk management models, and Monte Carlo simulations, R offers packages like QuantLib and fPortfolio.

4. Time Series Analysis: R provides specialised packages for time series analysis, including predict, TSA, and zoo, which let analysts forecast and analyse financial time series data as well as spot patterns, seasonality, and anomaly identification.

5. Quantitative Finance: Backtesting trading methods, examining market data, researching asset pricing, and creating algorithmic trading systems are just a few of the quantitative finance jobs for which R is frequently utilised.

Python in Financial Analytics:

1. Data Manipulation and Analysis: Python is a great tool for cleaning, manipulating, and analysing data. Its libraries, such as Pandas and NumPy, enable analysts to carry out operations including data aggregation, filtering, transformation, and financial metric computation.

2. Machine Learning: Predictive models in financial analytics, such as credit scoring, fraud detection, stock price prediction, and customer segmentation, are built using Python's robust machine learning packages, such as scikit-learn, TensorFlow, and PyTorch.

3. Quantitative Analysis: In quantitative finance, Python is being utilised more and more for tasks like volatility modelling, risk management, portfolio optimisation, and derivative pricing. R-like functionalities for quantitative analysis can be found in libraries like PyQuantLib and QuantLib.

4. Web Scraping and Data Acquisition: Python's flexibility makes it a valuable tool for gathering financial data for additional analysis from a variety of sources, including websites, databases, and APIs.

5. Financial Visualisation: Analysts can generate aesthetically appealing charts, graphs, and dashboards to effectively communicate financial information by using Python's visualisation tools, such as Matplotlib, Seaborn, and Plotly.

6. Algorithmic Trading: Because of its speed, versatility, and vast libraries for financial analysis and trading, Python is widely used in algorithmic trading and quantitative finance for creating trading strategies, carrying out trades, and analysing market data.

In the financial sector, R and Python are both commonly used. Which one to use relies on a number of criteria, including the particulars of the project, the preferences of the analysts or data scientists, and the organization's current infrastructure. Utilising the advantages of both languages, many firms even combine R and Python for various financial analytics applications.

Financial analytics using Bloomberg Terminal

The financial industry makes extensive use of Bloomberg Terminal, a potent instrument for market data, news, research, and analytics. Financial professionals, such as traders, analysts, portfolio managers, and researchers, find it invaluable as it offers up-to-date and historical data on financial instruments, economic indicators, news, and analysis. The Bloomberg Terminal is utilised in financial analytics in the following ways:

1. Market Data Access:

   A wide range of market data, such as stock prices, bond yields, commodity prices, foreign exchange rates, and more, are available through the Bloomberg Terminal. Users are able to do quantitative analysis and analyse market patterns by retrieving historical and real-time data for financial instruments across many asset classes.

2.   Financial Analysis Tools:

Bloomberg offers financial modelling, technical analysis, and fundamental analysis as part of its analytical toolkit. Bloomberg's unique analytics enable users to analyse financial statements, assess valuation indicators, evaluate corporate performance, and do peer comparisons.

3.   News and Research:

Bloomberg Terminal offers current news feeds, research summaries, and analysis from reliable sources in addition to Bloomberg News. In order to make wise investment selections, financial professionals can keep up with market-moving events, economic changes, company announcements, and geopolitical news.

4.   Portfolio Management:

Bloomberg provides real-time tracking and analysis capabilities for users' investment portfolios. To assist with investing, users can track portfolio performance, evaluate asset allocation, examine risk metrics, and create personalized reports.

5.   Data Visualisation:

Charts, graphs, and dashboards can be created to display market trends, correlations, and performance measures using Bloomberg's data visualisation tools. Customised visualisations can be shared with clients or coworkers to help with decision-making and communication.

6.   Trading and Execution:

The Bloomberg Terminal facilitates trading in a variety of asset types, such as derivatives, equities, fixed income, and currencies. Through the Bloomberg platform, users can access liquidity pools, execute transactions immediately, and use sophisticated trading algorithms for the best possible execution.

7.   Economic Analysis:

Bloomberg offers a wealth of information on the economy, including projections for GDP growth, inflation rates, central bank policies, and macroeconomic indicators. Users are able to evaluate how economic factors affect financial markets and use economic trends to inform their investment selections.

8.   Risk Management:

Value-at-risk (VaR) analysis, stress testing, and scenario analysis are just a few of the risk management tools that Bloomberg Terminal customers can employ to evaluate the risk in their portfolios. Users are able to recognise possible dangers in their portfolios and reduce risk exposure by taking the necessary actions.

For financial professionals, the Bloomberg Terminal acts as a central hub since it gives them access to a multitude of market data, news, research, and analytical tools that are necessary for financial analysis and decision-making. Because of its extensive feature set, it is a vital tool for anyone working in the investment industry that uses financial analytics.

Interface of Financial Analytics in Technical Analysis

Technical Analysis

Based on past price data, trade volume, and other market indicators, technical analysis is a technique used to assess and forecast future price movements of financial assets, such as stocks, commodities, currencies, or indexes. In contrast to fundamental analysis, which is centred on the financial and economic aspects of a company, technical analysis mainly looks at price charts and patterns in order to spot trends and possible trading opportunities.

Concepts in Technical Analysis:

1. Price charts: Line charts:

The most basic type that display an asset's closing prices over a certain time span. The following the example of a line chart for stock price movements. The High, Low, Open and Close share prices are recorded in the excel initially. The same would be depicted in the form of line chart as shown below.

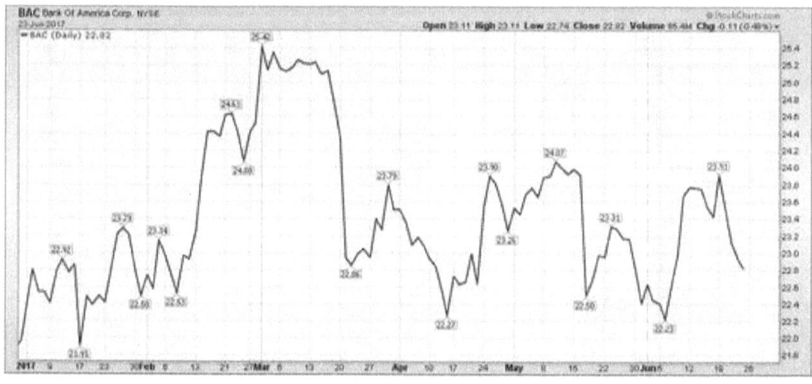

Bar charts:

This chart shows each period's open, high, low, and closing prices in the form of bar diagram as shown below.

Candlestick charts:

They display the price activity across each time period (e.g., daily) and are comparable to bar charts, but they provide additional visual information.

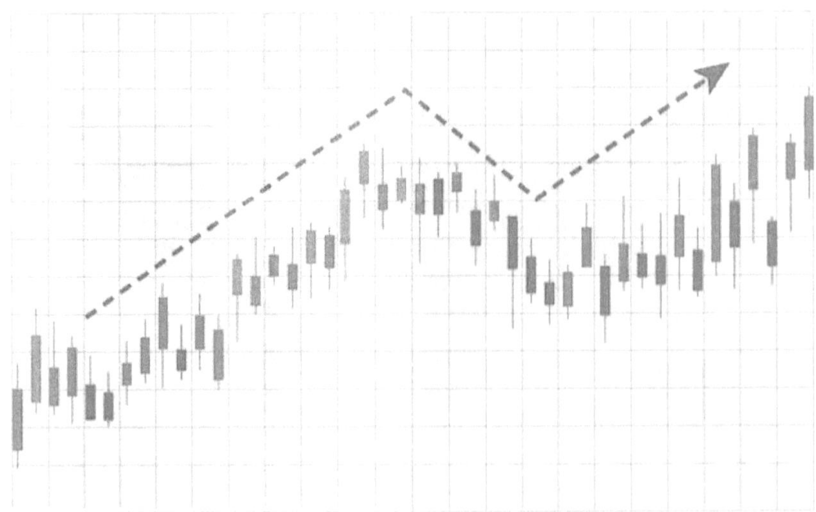

2. Trends:

Uptrend:

An upward trend is a sequence of higher highs and higher lows that point to an increase in prices.

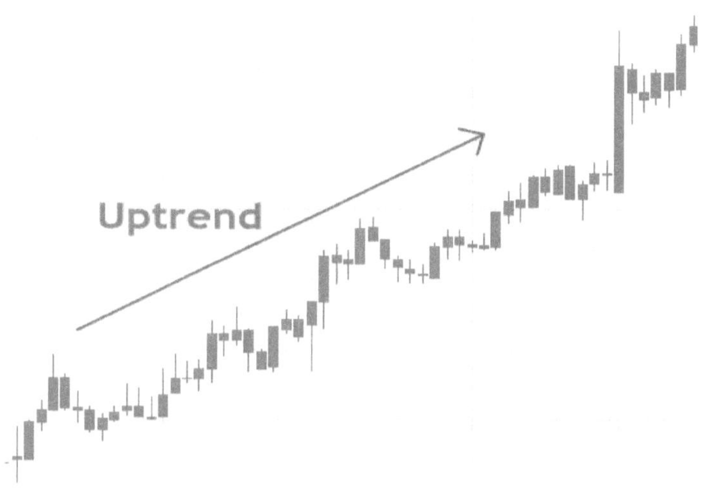

Downtrend:

A sequence of lower highs and lower lows that point to a declining price trend is known as a downtrend.

Sideways:

Price movement that is range-bound or sideways without a discernible rise or downturn.

3. Support and Resistance:

Support: The price point at which an asset usually stops declining and starts to rise again. It is seen as a price-supporting "floor."

Resistance is the point at a price where an asset usually stops increasing and starts to decline. It is regarded as a price-resistant "ceiling."

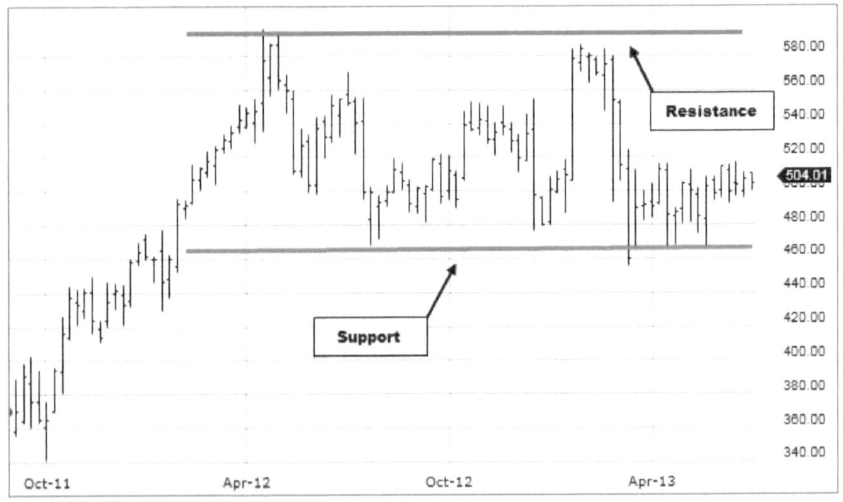

4. Technical Indicators:

Moving Averages:

A line used to normalise price data in order to determine the trend's direction. Simple Moving Average (SMA) and Exponential Moving Average (EMA) are two popular forms.

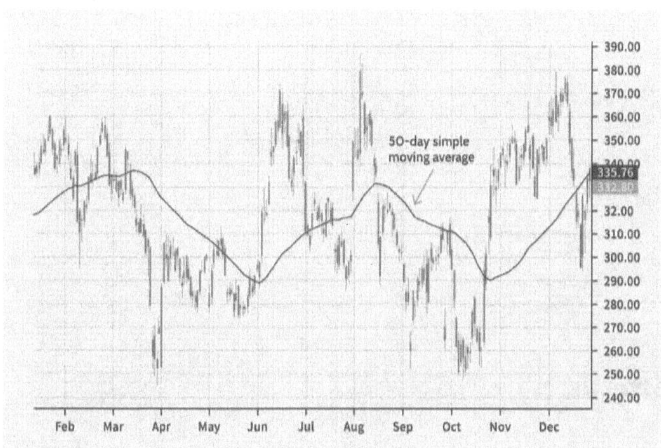

Relative Strength Index (RSI):

An oscillator of momentum that gauges the rate and direction of price changes; usually used to pinpoint overbought or oversold situations. Macd, or moving average convergence-divergence, a momentum indicator that tracks trends and displays the correlation between two price moving averages for an asset.

Bollinger Bands:

A moving average and two standard deviations (upper and lower bands) away from it make up this volatility indicator.

Graph Patterns:

Head and Shoulders:

A reversal pattern indicating a shift in the direction of the trend.

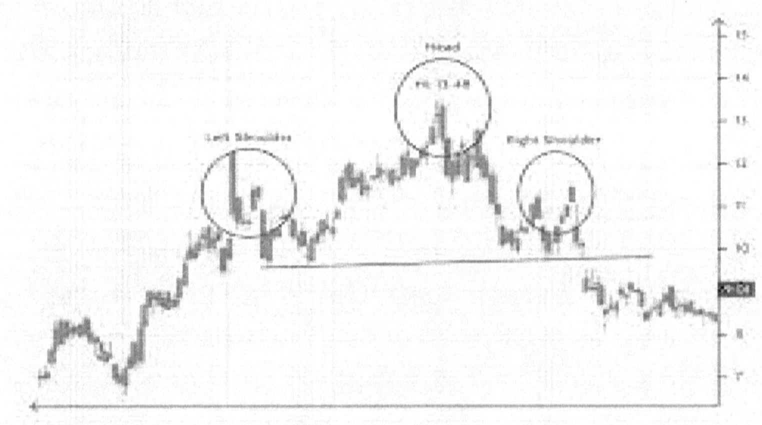

Double Top/Bottom:

Patterns that indicate a change in direction following two tests of the same degree of support or resistance.

Triangles:

As price enters a narrower range, patterns begin to form that suggest possible breakouts.

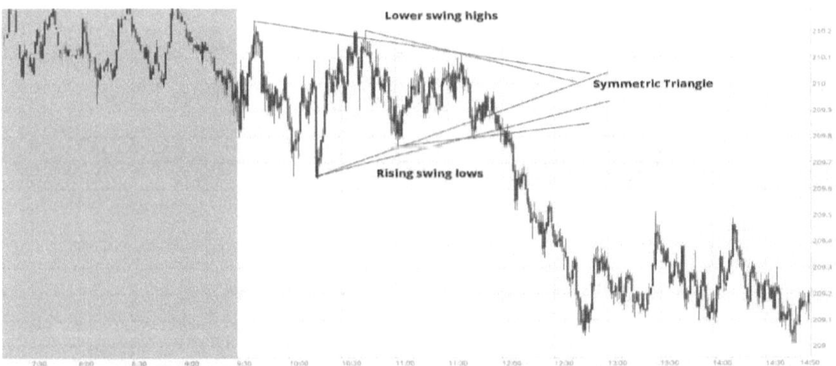

Analysis of Volume:

Understanding the strength or weakness of a price movement can be gained by analysing trading volume, which is the quantity of shares or contracts traded. An increase in price on high volume, for instance, is regarded as more important than on low volume.

Trends:

To determine the trend's direction, draw lines on price charts that join two or more price points. These lines have the power to either support or oppose.

Fibonacci Retracement:

A technique that uses the Fibonacci ratios (23.6%, 38.2%, 50%, 61.8%, and 100%) to calculate the distance between a notable high and low in order to detect possible reversal levels.

The Technical Analysis Theory:

Everything Is Discounted by Market Action. Technical analysts think that the price of an asset already considers all of the information that is currently available (such as economic statistics, political events, and earnings reports).

Prices Move in Trends:

Once a trend starts, it's more likely to stay that way than go the other way. The goal of technical analysis is to spot these movements early.

History Repetition Is Common:

Because of the tendency of the market to repeat itself, price patterns and movements can be used to forecast future price changes.

Application of Technical Analysis:

Traders and investors frequently employ technical analysis to:

Determine the points of entrance and exit for transactions. Ascertain the general attitude of the market.

Combine with other analytical techniques, such fundamental analysis, to produce a better trading strategy.

Technical analysis can be applied to any asset with historical trading data, making it a versatile tool in financial markets.

Interface between technical Analysis and Financial Analytics:

Technical analysis does make use of financial data, but mostly in a complementary way. Technical analysis is a technique used by investors and traders to assess past price data, trading volumes, and different technical indicators in order to forecast and assess future price movements of financial assets (such stocks, currencies, or commodities). In contrast, a wider range of instruments and methods for examining financial data are included in financial analytics, which can incorporate elements of both technical and fundamental analysis.

Data Processing and Collection as a Means of Supporting Technical Analysis in Financial Analytics

Technical analysis requires the collection and processing of enormous amounts of historical price data, which is a task associated with financial analytics. Traders can use it to examine correlations, trends, and patterns across time.

Real-Time Data Analysis: By processing real-time market data, sophisticated financial analytics tools help traders make prompt judgements based on the most recent changes in prices and market conditions.

Technical Measures

Creation of Indicators: Technical indicators like Bollinger Bands, MACD (Moving Average Convergence Divergence), RSI (Relative Strength Index), and moving averages can be created and customised using financial analytics. The statistical and quantitative study of price data serves as the foundation for these indicators.

Back testing Indicators:

Traders can evaluate the efficacy of technical indicators and improve their trading methods by applying them to historical data using financial analytics.

Identification of Patterns Chart Patterns:

Head and shoulders, double tops and bottoms, and triangles are examples of frequent chart patterns that may be found using financial analytics tools. These patterns are important parts of technical analysis.

Algorithmic Pattern Detection:

Technical analysis can be completed more quickly and accurately by automating the detection of these patterns using advanced analytics approaches such as machine learning.

Measurement and Evaluation

Statistical Analysis: Price distributions, volatility, and correlations between various financial instruments are all examined using statistical techniques in financial analytics. Technical analysis relies heavily on this data, particularly when determining the probability of specific price movements.

Quantitative Models: To forecast price changes, optimise trading tactics, and control risk, traders might use financial analytics to build quantitative models. Technical analysis indicators are frequently used in these models as a component of a larger analytical framework

Risk Management:

Financial analytics makes it possible to analyse asset volatility, which aids traders in determining the level of risk involved in a certain technical trading strategy. Technical analysts frequently employ volatility indicators, including the Average True Range (ATR), to size positions and set stop-loss orders.

Scenario Analysis and Stress Testing:

Trading techniques based on technical analysis can be stress tested and several market scenarios can be simulated using analytics tools. This aids traders in comprehending the possible benefits and drawbacks of their methods in various market scenarios.

Trading Algorithms and Automation:

Automated Trading Systems: Technical analysis-based trading decisions are automated by algorithmic trading systems, for which financial analytics is essential. Upon meeting predetermined thresholds, including crossing moving averages or hitting specific price points, these systems have the ability to execute transactions.

Trading Algorithm Optimisation:

Analytics tools are useful for fine-tuning the parameters of trading algorithms so that the trader's objectives and risk tolerance are met.

Sentiment Analysis:

Market Sentiment:

By analysing data from social media, news sources, and market sentiment indices, financial analytics can include sentiment analysis. Although sentiment research is more closely associated with fundamental analysis, it can serve as a valuable supplement to technical analysis by offering insights into the psychology of the market that may impact price movements.

Conclusion:

Financial analytics offers the instruments and methods to increase the efficacy of technical analysis, even if technical analysis typically employs past price data and chart patterns to inform trading decisions. Traders may handle enormous volumes of data, create and test indicators, control risk, and even automate trading methods by utilising financial analytics. Technical analysis that incorporates financial analytics makes decisions more data-driven and well-informed, which increases the likelihood of success in the financial markets.

Predictive Analytics in Finance

Using data, statistical algorithms, and machine learning approaches, predictive analytics in finance forecasts future events, trends, and behaviours in the financial sector. To forecast financial markets, investment performance, customer behaviour, risk management, and other financial activities, it makes use of both historical and current data. Predictive analytics is used in the following financial domains:

1. Stock Market Forecasting:

    Using historical price data, trade volume, technical indicators, and macroeconomic variables as a basis, predictive analytics is utilised to forecast stock prices, market trends, and volatility. Regression analysis, time series forecasting, and neural networks are a few examples of machine learning techniques that are used to find trends and estimate future moves in stocks.

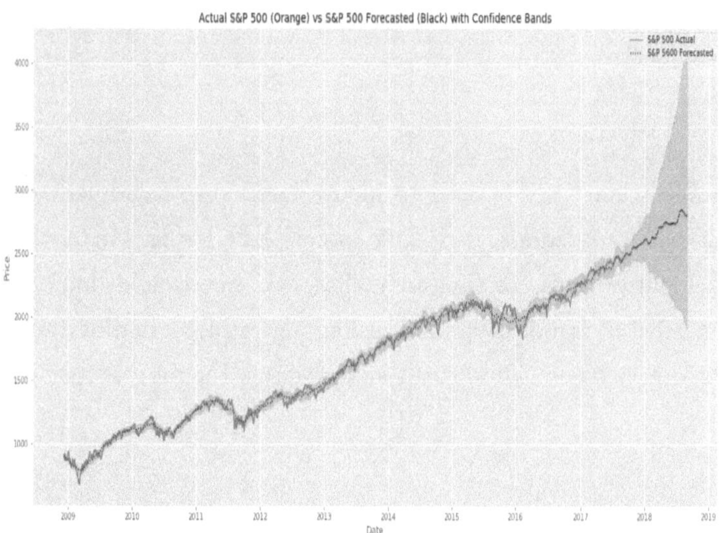

2. Credit Risk Assessment:

By forecasting the chance of default or delinquency for specific borrowers or loan portfolios, predictive analytics is essential to the assessment of credit risk. To evaluate creditworthiness and make lending decisions, credit scoring models—such as ensemble methods, decision trees, and logistic regression—analyze borrower data, credit history, financial ratios, and macroeconomic factors.

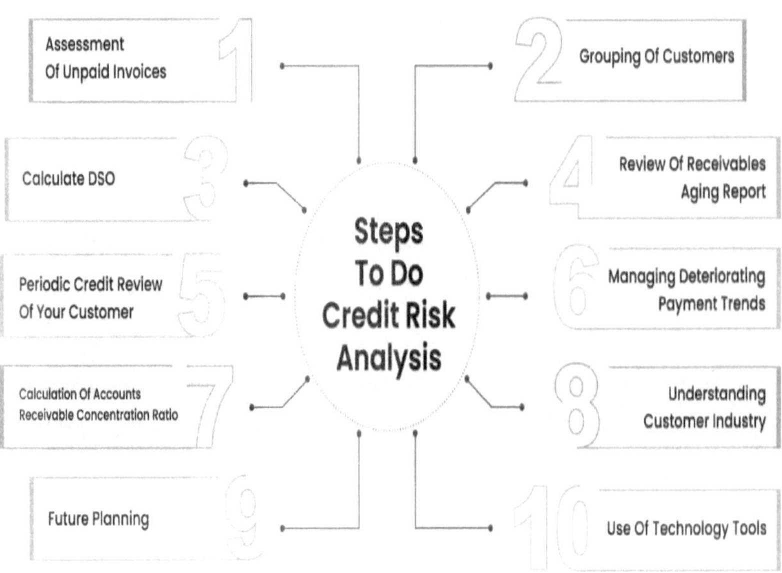

3. Fraud Detection:

Predictive analytics is used to identify and stop fraudulent activity in financial transactions, including money laundering, credit card fraud, and identity theft. To find anomalies, odd trends, and dubious activity suggestive of fraud, machine learning algorithms examine transactional data, user behaviour, and past fraud patterns. The process is as follows:

a) Gathering and Combining Data:

Information is gathered from a number of sources, including past fraud incidents, user profiles, transaction records, and device information. Models can capture behaviours across several channels and identify disparities when they have access to a comprehensive dataset. For instance, information about device kind, payment methods, geolocation, and transaction history are all integrated in banking.

b) Pre-processing and Data Cleaning

To eliminate discrepancies and standardise formats, data is cleaned and pre-processed. It increases prediction reliability by ensuring that model input data is reliable and consistent. Examples include standardizing time stamps, eliminating duplicate entries, and filling in missing values.

c) Feature engineering:

It is the process of creating or extracting pertinent features in order to identify trends that might point to fraud. This assists models in recognizing important indicators including transaction volume, frequency, and location consistency.

For instance, figuring out the typical transaction size, frequency, or velocity of transactions across brief periods of time.

d) Developing Predictive Models and Training:

Both supervised and unsupervised learning techniques are used to train machine learning models on historical data. Learning to distinguish between honest and dishonest behaviour and forecasting fresh data are the goals.

Examples include unsupervised learning (without labelled data) that uses clustering techniques like k-means to identify anomalies and supervised learning (with labelled fraud data) with models like logistic regression or decision trees.

e) Modelling Methods for Fraud Identification:

Finding odd patterns that diverge from typical behaviour is known as anomaly detection. The methods include statistical outlier detection, isolation forests, and clustering (k-means). Transactions are categorised as either fraudulent or lawful using classification models. Neural networks, SVMs, Random Forest, and Gradient Boosting are used as methods to detect frauds. In order to identify fraud rings, network analysis looks at the relationships between entities, such as people, accounts, or devices. Social network analysis or graph analysis are also popularly used.

f) Instantaneous Evaluation and Decision-Making:

Real-time scoring of transactions is used to detect possibly fraudulent activity. The goal is to promptly flag or halt suspicious transactions so that prompt action can be taken. For instance, banks employ fraud scoring algorithms to notify or prevent transactions that exceed a predetermined level of risk.

g) Model Tracking and Ongoing Enhancement

To accommodate emerging fraud trends, models are routinely reviewed and modified. The goal is to keep the model functional even when scammers change their strategies. Example: Using feedback from fresh fraud cases and retraining models on recent data on a regular basis.

4. **Customer Segmentation and Targeting:**

    Financial institutions can customise goods, services, and marketing campaigns for particular customer categories by using predictive analytics to segment clients according to their needs, preferences, and behaviours. Customer data is analysed by clustering algorithms, like k-means and hierarchical clustering, to find homogeneous groups and target them with recommendations and offers that are specifically tailored to them.

5. **Forecasting and Financial Planning:**

    By projecting future revenues, costs, cash flows, and financial performance based on historical data, industry trends, and business drivers, predictive analytics helps with financial planning and forecasting. For the sake of budgeting, resource allocation, and strategic decision-making, time series forecasting models, including ARIMA, exponential smoothing, and Prophet, evaluate past financial data to produce both short- and long-term projections.

6. **Algorithmic Trading:**

    To create trading strategies, spot lucrative trade opportunities, and improve trade execution, predictive analytics is frequently applied in algorithmic trading. Machine learning algorithms are utilised in financial markets to produce buy/sell signals, manage risk, and maximise trading profits by analysing market data, news sentiment, and trading indications.

7. Portfolio Management: To optimise portfolio allocations, control risk, and optimise investment returns, predictive analytics is used in portfolio management. Value at Risk (VaR) and Conditional Value at Risk (CVaR) are two examples of risk forecasting models that use historical asset returns and volatility to predict the possible downside risk of investment portfolios and guide asset allocation choices.

8. Insurance Underwriting:

    To evaluate the risk of insuring people or assets and establish fair premiums, predictive analytics is employed in insurance underwriting. In order to forecast the possibility of future insurance claims and make underwriting choices, machine learning algorithms examine client data, claims history, and risk factors.

    In a dynamic and competitive financial world, predictive analytics helps financial institutions to manage risks effectively, make data-driven choices, optimise business operations, and improve client experiences. Organisations may improve decision-making, get insightful knowledge, and spur innovation in the financial sector by utilising sophisticated analytics approaches and utilising data.

Case Study: Predictive Analytics-Based Stock Market Forecasting

Background: Stock market analysis and portfolio management are the areas of expertise for financial company ABC Investment Management. Through the use of predictive analytics, the company hopes to improve its stock market forecasting abilities and produce alpha for its clientele by making data-driven investing decisions.

Problems:

1. Market Volatility:

   The stock market is very volatile, which makes it difficult to forecast future price fluctuations with any degree of accuracy.

2. Information Overload:

   It might be challenging to spot pertinent signals and trends due to the abundance of financial data available, which includes historical price data, corporate financials, news sentiment, and economic indicators.

3. Risk Management:

   Since inaccurate forecasts might result in monetary losses, the company needs to have a strong risk management program.

4. Competition:

   Developing a competitive edge in the fiercely competitive financial sector calls for creative and advanced forecasting models.

Solution:

ABC Investment Management uses predictive analytics to put into practice a stock market forecasting framework:

1. Data Collection and Preprocessing:

   Gathers information from a variety of sources, such as news items, historical price data, fundamental indicators, sentiment analysis on social media, and macroeconomic indicators. Pre-processes and cleans the data to fill in missing values, eliminate noise, and harmonise formats.

2. Feature engineering:

   Finds pertinent characteristics and factors, such as sentiment scores, trading volumes, moving averages, price momentum, and earnings releases, that could affect stock prices. Develops new features or modifies current features to identify significant trends and connections in the data.

3. Model Selection and Training:

    Chooses suitable machine learning techniques, such as gradient boosting, random forests, decision trees, and linear regression, for stock market forecasting. Creates training and testing sets from the data, then uses past data to train the predictive models to find trends and connections between stock prices and feature values.

4. Model Validation and Evaluation:

    Assesses the prediction models' performance using suitable evaluation measures, like mean absolute error (MAE), root mean square error (RMSE), or mean square error (MSE). To guarantee the models' resilience and ability to generalize to new data, they are validated using cross-validation or out-of-sample data.

5. Integration and Deployment:

    Incorporates stock market projections into portfolio design, asset allocation, and other investment decision-making processes by integrating the predictive models into the process. Tracks the performance of the models over time and changes them often to account for shifting market dynamics and conditions.

Findings:

1. Enhanced Forecast Accuracy:

    ABC Investment Management produces more dependable projections of future price movements and trends by attaining higher forecast accuracy in the stock market.

2. Improved Risk-adjusted Returns:

   Predictive analytics-driven data-driven investment decisions produce better risk-adjusted returns for client portfolios, surpassing peers trategies and benchmarks.

3. Improved Risk Management:

   To reduce downside risk and safeguard client funds from unfavourable market fluctuations, the company uses strong risk management strategies.

4. Competitive Advantage:

   By utilizing predictive analytics to find lucrative investment opportunities and provide clients with better investment performance, ABC Investment Management obtains a competitive advantage in the industry.

   In summary, this case study illustrates how ABC investing Management improved its stock market predicting skills and boosted investing success by utilising predictive analytics. Through the utilisation of sophisticated analytical tools and data, the company managed risk more efficiently, made better investment decisions, and outperformed rivals in a competitive and ever-changing financial market.

Case Study: Using Predictive Analytics to Assess Credit Risk

XYZ Bank is a well-known lender that provides a range of credit products, such as credit cards, mortgages, and personal loans. By utilising predictive analytics, the bank hopes to improve the accuracy of its credit risk assessment procedures and reduce the likelihood of default by assessing loan applicants' creditworthiness.

Problems:

1. High Default Rates:

   XYZ Bank is confronted with a problem of a high default rate among loan applicants, which contributes to a rise in credit losses and unstable finances.

2. Manual Underwriting Procedures:

A large portion of the bank's credit assessment procedures are based on manual assessments, which are labor-intensive and prone to bias.

3. Limited Data Integration:

The storage of data in several systems, such as application forms, financial statements, and credit bureaus, makes it difficult to do effective analysis.

4. Regulatory Compliance:

To maintain capital adequacy ratios and regulatory compliance, proper credit risk assessment is necessary in order to comply with regulatory norms, such as Basel III.

Resolution:

XYZ Bank uses predictive analytics to put into practice a framework for credit risk assessment:

1. Integration and Preparation of Data:

    Combines information from a variety of sources, including external sources like social media and internet transactions, internal databases, and credit bureaus. Prepares the data for analysis by cleaning and preprocessing it to eliminate errors, add missing values, and standardize data formats.

2. Engineering and Feature Selection:

    Determines pertinent characteristics and factors, such as credit scores, income levels, employment status, debt-to-income ratios, and payment histories, that may have an impact on credit risk. Works with subject matter experts to develop new features or modify current ones in order to capture intricate linkages and patterns in the data.

3.   Model Development:

Chooses machine learning techniques (e.g., logistic regression, decision trees, random forests, or gradient boosting machines) that are appropriate for assessing credit risk. Uses historical data to train prediction models to identify trends and connections between attributes and credit outcomes, such as default or non-default.

4.   Model Validation and Evaluation:

Assesses the predictive models' performance using metrics including area under the receiver operating characteristic curve (AUC-ROC), accuracy, precision, and recall. To guarantee the models' resilience and ability to generalize to fresh data, they are validated using holdout datasets or cross-validation methods.

5.   Deployment and Monitoring:

Automates credit risk assessments for loan applications by integrating the predictive models into the bank's credit decision-making process. Tracks the performance of the models over time and makes frequent adjustments to them to enhance predicted accuracy and adjust to shifting market conditions.

Findings:

1.   Increased Credit Decision Accuracy:

XYZ Bank makes better credit risk assessments, which results in better lending decisions and a decrease in loan application default rates.

2.   Increased Efficiency:

Automating credit risk assessment procedures increases operational efficiency by streamlining loan origination workflows and lowering manual labour.

3. Risk Mitigation:

    The bank can reduce credit losses by using risk mitigation techniques, such as higher interest rates, lower credit limits, or collateral requirements, by precisely identifying high-risk loan applicants.

4. Regulatory Compliance:

    The bank can maintain capital adequacy ratios and regulatory compliance by accurately assessing credit risk, which ensures compliance with regulatory regulations.

In summary, this case study shows how XYZ Bank used predictive analytics to improve the quality of its credit risk assessment procedures, which resulted in better lending decisions, lower default rates, and more compliance with regulations. The bank was able to improve results for the organisation and its clients by optimising its credit risk management procedures and utilising data-driven insights and sophisticated analytics approaches.

Case Study: Implementation of Algorithmic Trading

Hedge fund Alpha Investment Management focusses on quantitative trading techniques. By utilising modern analytics and machine learning techniques in its algorithmic trading tactics, the company hopes to improve both its trading performance and efficiency.

Problems:

1. Market Complexity:

    Finding lucrative trading opportunities is difficult due to the high volatility, intricate dynamics, and massive amounts of data that characterize financial markets.

2. Manual Trading Processes:

    The speed and scalability of trading activities are constrained by the laborious and human bias- prone nature of traditional manual trading processes.

3. Competition:

    To obtain an advantage in the fiercely competitive financial sector, one must employ complex and creative trading techniques that can surpass conventional methods.

4. Regulatory Compliance:

    Rules pertaining to market integrity, order execution, and risk management, among other regulations, must be followed by algorithmic trading operations.

Resolution:

Alpha Investment Management uses machine learning and sophisticated analytics to develop an algorithmic trading framework:

1. Gathering and preprocessing data:

    Gathers real-time market data from a variety of exchanges and data providers, such as price quotations, trading volumes, order book data, and news sentiment. Prepares the data for analysis by standardizing data formats, eliminating noise, and filling in missing values.

2. Strategy Development:

    To find successful trading opportunities, develops algorithmic trading strategies based on technical indicators, quantitative models, and machine learning algorithms.

3.   Generates trading signals and makes buy/sell choices by utilising statistical arbitrage, trend- following, mean reversion, and sentiment analysis approaches.

4.   Backtesting and Optimisation:

Utilising past market data, backtests trading methods to assess performance, examine risk-adjusted returns, and optimise parameters. Uses optimisation approaches, parameter tuning, and sensitivity analysis to improve strategy robustness and performance in a variety of market scenarios.

5.   Model Implementation:

Integrates real-time data feeds, execution algorithms, and risk management controls into the trading infrastructure of the company in order to implement the algorithmic trading models. Automates trade execution, reduces latency, and optimises order routing for optimal execution by utilising trading platforms, APIs, and execution algorithms.

6.   Monitoring and Risk Management:

Tracks important performance indicators, including profitability, drawdowns, turnover, and the Sharpe ratio, while keeping an eye on the real-time performance of algorithmic trading method. Uses risk management tools to control downside risk, such as circuit breakers, stop-loss orders, and position limitations.

Results:

1.   Better Trading Performance:

When compared to conventional manual trading techniques, Alpha Investment Management outperforms peer strategies and benchmarks in terms of trading performance and risk-adjusted returns.

2. Enhanced Efficiency:

   The company may take advantage of transient trading opportunities thanks to algorithmic trading automation, which simplifies trading processes, lowers manual labor, and speeds up execution.

3. Better Risk Management:

   The company can efficiently manage downside risk, avert significant losses, and safeguard money in erratic market conditions thanks to risk management controls and monitoring technologies.

4. Regulatory Compliance:

   In compliance with regulatory norms, algorithmic trading activities guarantee market integrity, order transparency, and investor protection.

   In summary, this case study demonstrates how Alpha Investment Management improved trading efficiency, performance, and risk management skills by utilising algorithmic trading tactics. The company was able to create complex trading models, automate trade execution, and gain a competitive edge in the quick-moving and dynamic financial markets by utilising advanced analytics and machine learning approaches.

Case Study: Optimising Portfolio Management

High-net-worth individuals and institutional clients' portfolios are managed by Gamma Capital Management, an investment firm. By employing cutting-edge analytics and optimisation strategies, the company hopes to improve its portfolio management procedures and optimise returns while prudently controlling risk.

Problems:

1. Diverse Client Objectives:

    It might be difficult to customize investment strategies to meet the demands of each unique client at Gamma Capital because the firm manages portfolios for a range of clients with different risk tolerances, time horizons, and financial objectives.

2. Market Volatility:

    The high levels of volatility seen in the financial markets make it challenging to forecast changes in asset prices and adjust portfolio allocations appropriately.

3. Regulatory Compliance:

    The management of portfolios must adhere to legal and regulatory obligations, including risk management standards, investing guidelines, and fiduciary duties.

4. Performance Pressure:

    The company is under pressure to minimize volatility and drawdowns while outperforming benchmarks and delivering competitive returns.

Solution:

Using cutting-edge analytics and optimization methods, Gamma Capital Management puts into practice a framework   for portfolio management optimization.

1. Client Profiling and Risk Assessment:

    This process involves creating a client profile that considers their time horizon, investment goals, liquidity requirements and other pertinent variables. Identifies relevant risk measures, such as Value at Risk (VaR), projected shortfall, and maximum drawdown, and conducts risk assessment to quantify risk preferences and restrictions.

2.   Asset Allocation Optimization:

This technique optimizes portfolio allocations based on predicted returns, volatilities, correlations, and risk preferences by utilising mean-variance optimisation, contemporary portfolio theory, and asset pricing models. It takes into account restrictions including regulatory limitations, sector allocations, asset class exposures, and liquidity needs.

3.   Diversity Techniques:

To lower portfolio risk and improve risk-adjusted returns, employ diversity techniques such as asset class diversification, regional diversification and sector rotation. It makes use of strategies for risk parity, minimum variance, and maximum diversification to maximize portfolio efficiency and gets the ideal level of diversification.

4.   Performance Monitoring and Rebalancing:

Tracks important performance measures, including information ratio, total return, Sharpe ratio, and tracking error, monitors portfolio performance in real-time.Uses dynamic portfolio rebalancing techniques to modify portfolio allocations in response to shifting customer needs, fresh information and shifting market conditions.

Findings:

1.   Improved Risk-Adjusted Returns:

Gamma Capital Management outperforms rival strategies and benchmarks in generating higher risk-adjusted returns for client portfolios while skillfully minimizing downside risk.

2. Customized Solutions:

   Personalized portfolio management techniques cater to each client's particular requirements and tastes.

3. Enhanced Efficiency:

   Automation and optimization strategies minimize manual labor, enhance operational efficiency and expedite portfolio management procedures.

4. Regulatory Compliance:

   Activities related to portfolio management adhere to regulatory norms, guaranteeing responsibility, transparency, and investor protection.

In summary, this case study demonstrates how Gamma Capital Management used portfolio management optimisation methodologies to improve investment performance, efficiently manage risk, and provide clients with tailored solutions. The company was able to create complex portfolio management strategies, automate decision-making procedures, and gain competitive advantages in the difficult and dynamic investment market by utilising advanced analytics and optimisation approaches.

Case Study: Optimising Insurance Underwriting

As one of the top suppliers of insurance goods, Delta Insurance Company offers health, property, and life insurance. By using advanced analytics and machine learning approaches, the company hopes to improve its underwriting procedures and increase profitability by accurately assessing risk, pricing policies competitively, and increasing profitability.

Problems:

1. Accurate Risk Assessment:

   Delta Insurance has trouble determining the risk involved in providing insurance for people or property, which can cause insurance products to be overpriced or underpriced.

2. Manual Underwriting Processes:

   Due to their heavy reliance on manual judgements, traditional underwriting techniques are labor-intensive, arbitrary and susceptible to bias.

3. Data Complexity:

   Insurance underwriting necessitates the examination of substantial amounts of data, including risk factors, medical records, claims history, and customer information.

4. Competitive Pressure:

   The insurance sector is extremely competitive, and obtaining a competitive advantage necessitates using cutting-edge, data-driven methods for risk assessment and underwriting. Solution: Using cutting-edge analytics and machine learning, Delta Insurance puts into practice an insurance underwriting optimization platform.

Solution:

1. Integration and Preparation of Data:

   Combines information from a variety of sources, including social media, credit bureaus, medical records, claims databases and consumer applications.

   Prepares the data for analysis by standardizing data formats, removing duplicates, and validating and cleaning the information.

2. Risk Assessment Models:

    Using machine learning algorithms like logistic regression, random forests, gradient boosting, or neural networks, this section develops prediction models for risk assessment. Examines client information, past insurance claims, health information, and risk variables to forecast the possibility of insurance claims and determine whether applicants are insurable.

3. Predictive Underwriting:

    Makes use of predictive analytics to expedite approval procedures, increase productivity, and automate underwriting choices. Creates scoring models, decision trees, or underwriting procedures that divide applicants into risk groups and establish suitable premium amounts.

4. Fraud Detection:

    Identifies questionable claims or fraudulent activity by applying anomaly detection algorithms, social network analysis, and text mining. Examines transaction patterns, behavioral indications, and claims data for abnormalities, discrepancies, or trends that might point to fraud.

5. Model Validation and Evaluation:

    Assesses underwriting model performance using metrics including area under the receiver operating characteristic curve (AUC-ROC), accuracy, precision, and recall. Verifies the models' resilience and generalizability using holdout datasets or cross-validation methods.

Results:

1. Improved Underwriting Accuracy:

    By increasing its risk assessment accuracy, Delta Insurance is able to make better underwriting judgements, lower claim losses, and increase profitability.

2. Increased Efficiency:

    Automating underwriting procedures increases operational efficiency by streamlining approval workflows and lowering manual labour.

3. Improved Risk Management:

    The organization may effectively manage underwriting risks, avoid insurance losses, and safeguard revenue with the help of accurate risk assessment and fraud detection.

4. Competitive Advantage:

    By utilizing cutting-edge analytics to enhance pricing tactics, streamline underwriting procedures, and provide better customer service, Delta Insurance obtains a competitive advantage in the industry.

In summary, this case study demonstrates how Delta Insurance used machine learning and advanced analytics to streamline its insurance underwriting procedures, precisely estimate risk, and increase profitability. The business was able to enhance decision-making, expedite underwriting processes, and obtain a competitive edge in the cutthroat insurance market by embracing automation and data-driven insights.

Chapter 11

Case Studies in Financial Analytics

Case Study: Using Financial Analytics to Enhance Investment Portfolio Performance

An international asset management company seeks to improve the performance of its investment portfolios by maintaining a broad array of holdings in a number of asset classes. The company looks after pension funds, high-net-worth individuals, and institutional clients' investments. The investing team uses financial analytics to optimise portfolio allocation, reduce risk, and provide clients with higher-than-average returns.

Problems:

1. Lack of Data-Driven Insights:

    The investment team makes judgements on portfolio management based on instinct and conventional techniques rather than methodical data-driven insights into risk factors, asset correlations, and market patterns.

2. Suboptimal Asset Allocation:

    In the absence of strong analytics, decisions about portfolio allocation are dependent on past performance and personal opinions, which results in missed opportunities and suboptimal asset allocations.

3. Risk Management Issues:

    The company is vulnerable to credit risk, liquidity risk, and market volatility due to inadequate risk assessment and monitoring. The company's capacity to proactively manage and reduce possible risks is hampered by the lack of sophisticated risk analytics.

4. Performance Evaluation:

To assess the efficacy of investment strategies, monitor portfolio performance, and inform clients of results, the firm does not have extensive performance measures and benchmarks.

Solution:

To solve the issues and improve portfolio management capabilities, the company uses a financial analytics framework.

1. Data Integration and Analysis:

    Combines information from a variety of sources, such as alternative data sets, financial statements, market data feeds and economic indicators. Cleanses, validates, and preprocesses the data to ensure accuracy and consistency. Makes use of sophisticated analytics tools and methods to draw conclusions and spot trends in the data, including machine learning algorithms, regression analysis, and time series modelling.

2. Portfolio Optimisation:

    To create effective portfolios, mean-variance optimisation, contemporary portfolio theory, and risk-parity techniques are used in asset allocation analysis. Considers variables like limitations, volatility, correlations, and predicted returns to optimise portfolio allocations and produce the required risk-return profiles. Uses dynamic asset allocation techniques that adjust to shifting investment goals and market conditions.

3. Risk Management:

    Creates analytics and risk models to measure and control several kinds of risks, such as credit, liquidity, and market risk. Uses Value at Risk (VaR) modelling, scenario analysis, and stress testing to evaluate the possible effects of unfavorable events on portfolio performance. Uses risk mitigation techniques to lower portfolio risk exposures, including as position sizing, diversification, and hedging.

4. Performance Metrics, Benchmarks, and Key Performance Indicators (KPIs) are defined in order to assess portfolio performance in relation to client goals and industry norms.

    Produces thorough performance reports and dashboards for monitoring peer comparisons, attribution analysis, risk-adjusted performance and portfolio returns. Offers clients frank and perceptive performance analysis.

Findings:

1. Improved Portfolio Performance:

    By using data-driven asset allocation strategies and risk management tactics, the company increases risk-adjusted returns and portfolio diversification.

2. Proactive Risk Management:

    During market downturns, the company can better detect and manage possible risks by utilizing advanced risk analytics, which increases portfolio stability and resilience.

3. Client happiness:

    Increased client trust and happiness are a result of transparent performance reporting and perceptive analytics, which promote client retention and company expansion.

Competitive Advantage:

By using financial analytics to generate better investment outcomes and set itself apart from rivals, the company gains a competitive edge in the market.

In summary, this case study shows how a multinational asset management company used financial analytics to maximise the performance of investment portfolios, successfully manage risks, and provide value to clients in a setting where markets are competitive. By adopting modern analytics skills and data-driven decision-making, the company placed itself up for long-term success and further expansion in the ever-changing asset management market.

Case Study: Financial Analytics for Risk Management

XYZ Bank is a well-known financial company that provides a variety of banking and financial services. XYZ Bank wants to use financial analytics to improve its risk management procedures and guarantee regulatory compliance while keeping an effective eye on risk management.

Problems:

1. Inadequate Risk Assessment:

    Credit risk, market risk, operational risk, and liquidity risk are just a few of the risks that XYZ Bank must effectively identify and measure.

2. Limited Capabilities for Risk Monitoring:

    The bank does not have strong instruments or processes in place to monitor risk exposures in real time or spot new hazards in its portfolio.

3. Compliance Requirements:

    Basel III, the Dodd-Frank Act, and Anti-Money Laundering (AML) regulations, among others, compel XYZ Bank to adhere to stringent compliance standards.

4. Risk Culture and Governance:

    To proactively manage risks and uphold the confidence of its stakeholders, XYZ Bank must have a solid framework for risk culture and governance.

Solution:

By utilising financial analytics, XYZ Bank establishes a thorough risk management framework:

1. Integration and Analysis of Data:

   - Combines information from both internal and external sources, such as regulatory reports, transaction data, customer data, and market data.

   - To guarantee correctness and consistency, the data is cleaned, validated, and pre- processed.

   - Makes use of cutting-edge analytics tools and methods to assess risk indicators and spot possible risks, including predictive modelling, machine learning algorithms, and scenario analysis.

2. Risk Management of Credit:

   - Creates analytics and credit scoring models to evaluate borrower creditworthiness and efficiently manage credit risk.

   - Estimates loss given default (LGD), computes exposure at default (EAD), and predicts default probabilities using historical data and predictive analytics.

   - Uses scenario analysis and stress testing to evaluate the effects of unfavourable economic situations.

3. Market Risk Management:

   - To quantify and control market risk exposures across trading and investment portfolios, Value at Risk (VaR) modelling and stress testing approaches are used.

   - Makes use of financial analytics to forecast market volatility, interest rate movements, and foreign currency variations as well as to evaluate previous market data and find correlations.

- Creates risk-reduction plans and hedging measures to reduce the effect of market swings on the bank's bottom line.

4. Operational Risk Management:

   - This involves identifying operational risk events and evaluating the possible effects they may have on the financial performance, operations, and reputation of the bank.

   - Uses risk control self-assessment (RCSA) procedures and key risk indicators (KRIs) to monitor and proactively reduce operational risks.

   - Makes use of scenario analysis and root cause analysis to pinpoint operational process flaws and enhance risk management procedures.

5. Liquidity Risk Management:

   - To evaluate the bank's capacity to meet its funding obligations under various circumstances, liquidity risk measures and stress testing models are developed.

   - Employs cash flow forecasts, funding gap analysis, and liquidity coverage ratio (LCR) computations to effectively handle exposure to liquidity risk and uphold sufficient liquidity reserves.

   - Puts procedures for managing liquidity risk and emergency funding in place to reduce risk and guarantee regulatory compliance.

Results:

1. Better Risk Assessment:

   XYZ Bank is able to make proactive risk management and decision-making by achieving more thorough and accurate risk assessments in the areas of credit, market, operational, and liquidity risk.

2. Improved Risk Monitoring:

With sophisticated analytics tools and dashboards, the bank has real-time visibility into risk exposures and emerging risks, allowing for prompt actions and risk mitigation strategies.

3. Regulatory Compliance:

By putting in place strong risk management procedures, reporting tools, and governance frameworks backed by financial analytics, XYZ Bank exhibits compliance with regulatory regulations.

4. Strengthened Risk Culture:

Financial analytics-cultivated strong risk culture and governance frameworks support proactive risk management, employee awareness, and accountability inside the company.

This case study demonstrates how XYZ Bank improved its risk management by using financial analytics.

Case Study: Financial Analytics-Based Performance Evaluation

Acme Asset Management is a top investment company that looks after high-net- worth individuals' and institutional clients' various asset portfolios. The company is dedicated to providing exceptional investment returns and is utilising financial analytics to improve its performance assessment tools.

Problems:

1. Absence of Comprehensive Performance measurements:

Acme Asset Management is unable to accurately track portfolio performance or assess the efficacy of its investment strategies due to the lack of a standardised set of performance measurements and benchmarks.

2. Limited Attribution Analysis:

   The company has difficulties determining which factors contribute to portfolio performance and evaluating their relative contributions, including market timing, security selection, and asset allocation choices.

3. Inadequate Peer Comparisons:

   Acme Asset Management cannot evaluate its competitive position in the market or compare its performance to that of peer companies because it does not have access to industry benchmarks or comparable data.

4. Client Reporting needs:

   The company must satisfy client reporting needs by offering clear, illuminating performance reports that highlight the benefits of its financial analytics and investment strategies.

Solution:

Acme Asset Management uses financial analytics to develop a framework for performance measurement:

1. Performance Metrics Definition:

   - Specifies and provides extensive range of performance indicators and benchmarks, such as tracking error, alpha, beta, information ratio, Sharpe ratio, and return on investment (ROI), to assess portfolio performance in various contexts.

   - Provides individualized performance reporting by customizing performance measures according to client goals, risk tolerance, and investment mandates.

2. Attribution Analysis:

   - To break down portfolio returns and pinpoint the causes of underperformance or outperformance, attribution analysis is carried out utilising factor models, regression analysis, and performance attribution approaches.

- Evaluates how decisions about asset allocation, choosing securities, and other elements affect portfolio performance, enabling well-informed choices and strategy improvement.

3. Peer Comparisons:

- To evaluate relative performance and pinpoint areas for improvement, benchmark portfolio performance against pertinent market indices, peer group averages, and industry benchmarks.

- Makes efficient use of peer analysis and comparative data to assess the firm's competitive position, set itself apart from the competition, and explain its value proposition to clients.

4. Client Reporting and Communication:

- Using financial analytics tools and visualisation techniques, creates detailed performance reports and client presentations that convey investment results, performance attribution, and portfolio insights.

- To improve client knowledge and engagement, offers clear and perceptive performance commentary that highlights important events, major performance factors, and the investment outlook

Results:

1. Improved Performance Measurement:

Acme Asset Management is able to assess portfolio performance more precisely and comprehensively along a number of parameters, which facilitates more intelligent decision-making and strategy optimisation.

2. Better Attribution Analysis:

    Through attribution analysis, the company obtains a greater understanding of the factors that influence portfolio performance, which enables more efficient resource allocation and investment strategy optimisation.

3. Insightful Peer Comparisons:

    Acme Asset Management compares its performance to those of its competitors in the industry as well as pertinent market indexes in order to pinpoint areas for improvement and difference.

4. Improved Client Communication:

    Clear and informative performance reports show how the firm's investment strategies and financial analytics skills bring value, which in turn builds client satisfaction and trust.

    To sum up, this case study demonstrates how Acme Asset Management improved performance measurement, attribution analysis, peer comparisons, and client reporting capabilities by utilising financial analytics. Through the adoption of advanced analytics approaches and data- driven insights, the business was able to evaluate portfolio performance and inform clients with improved efficacy, accountability, and transparency.

Case Study: Using Financial Analytics for Financial Planning and Forecasting

Based in the technology industry, BlueStar Corporation is a multinational corporation with a focus on consumer electronics development and production. The organisation uses financial analytics to generate data-driven insights and decision-making in an effort to enhance its financial planning and forecasting procedures.

Problems:

1. Inaccurate Forecasting:

    Because it has little insight into market trends, demand swings, and competitive dynamics, BlueStar Corporation has trouble predicting sales revenues, costs and cash flows.

2. Manual Processes:

    The financial planning process makes extensive use of subjective judgements, spreadsheet- based analysis, and manual data collecting, which can cause errors, inefficiencies, and delays in the decision-making process.

3. Lack of Scenario Analysis:

    To evaluate the possible effects of different market scenarios, prevailing economic conditions, and business uncertainties on financial performance, the organization lacks strong scenario analysis capabilities.

4. Dynamic Business Environment:

    In order to effectively respond to market dynamics, BlueStar Corporation must employ flexible and adaptable financial planning and forecasting procedures. This is because the company operates in a competitive and quickly evolving industry.

Solution:

BlueStar Corporation uses financial analytics to build a framework for financial planning and forecasting.

1. Statistics Integration and Analysis:

    - Combines information from external sources, such as market research reports, economic indicators, and industry benchmarks, with information from internal systems, such as production statistics, sales records, and financial statements.

- Makes use of financial analytics tools and procedures to clean, validate, and preprocess the data in order to guarantee correctness and consistency.

2. Predictive Analytics:

- This method forecasts sales revenues, expenses, and cash flows by using predictive modelling techniques like time series analysis, regression analysis, and machine learning algorithms.

- Uses market trends, seasonality considerations, historical data, and other pertinent information to provide projections that are accurate and trustworthy.

3. Scenario Analysis:

- This method evaluates the possible effects of different market circumstances, economic variables, and business scenarios on financial performance.

- Makes use of Monte Carlo simulations, stress testing methods, and sensitivity analysis to assess various hypotheses, risks, and results in various scenarios.

4. Dynamic Forecasting:

- Uses dynamic forecasting models that adjust in real-time to shifting market trends, competitive dynamics, and business situations.

- Updates financial estimates and modifies strategic plans in response to new information by utilising rolling forecasts and ongoing monitoring.

Results:

1. Increased Forecast Accuracy:

   BlueStar Corporation's financial predictions are more accurate and dependable, which facilitates better decision-making and strategic planning.

2. Improved Decision Support:

   Management can assess risks, consider alternative options, and allocate resources more efficiently with the use of data-driven insights and scenario analysis skills.

3. Agility and Adaptability:

   In a dynamic business environment, the organisation can react swiftly to shifting market conditions, reduce risks, and seize opportunities thanks to dynamic forecasting models and scenario analysis.

4. Productivity and Efficiency:

   Financial planning process automation and the incorporation of financial analytics tools minimise manual labour, optimise workflows, and boost organisational productivity.

To sum up, this case study demonstrates how BlueStar Corporation used financial analytics to boost decision-making in a fast-paced, cutthroat corporate climate, improve financial planning and forecasting procedures, and generate data-driven insights. The firm's financial planning and forecasting activities were made more accurate, agile, and efficient by adopting sophisticated analytics approaches and utilising real-time data. This helped the company position itself for long-term success and growth.

Case Study: Using Financial Analytics for Credit Scoring and Risk Assessment

XYZ Bank is a well-known financial company that provides a variety of loan and banking services. By utilising financial analytics to better credit decision-making and efficiently manage credit risk, the bank aims to improve its credit scoring and risk assessment procedures.

Problems:

1. Inaccurate Credit Decisions:

    XYZ Bank has trouble determining borrowers' creditworthiness, which raises the default rate and credit losses.

2. Manual Underwriting Procedures:

    The bank evaluates loan applications using subjective judgements, manual underwriting procedures, and a limited amount of data analysis, which results in inconsistent and inefficient credit decisions.

3. Limited Risk Predictability:

    To estimate the likelihood of a default, the bank does not have reliable credit scoring models or risk assessment tools.

4. Regulatory Compliance Requirements:

    XYZ Bank needs to adhere to regulations that require efficient credit risk management procedures and reporting capabilities, such as Basel III guidelines and Anti-Money Laundering (AML) regulations.

Solution:

XYZ Bank uses financial analytics to build a framework for credit rating and risk assessment:

1. Data Integration and Analysis:

   - Compiles information from both internal and external sources, such as financial statements, applicant records, credit bureau data, and loan performance statistics from the past.

   - Makes use of financial analytics tools and procedures to clean, validate, and preprocess the data in order to guarantee correctness and consistency.

5. Models of Credit Scoring:

   - Creates predictive credit scoring models to evaluate borrower creditworthiness utilising statistical methods, machine learning algorithms, and credit risk indicators.

   - Uses a variety of factors, including debt-to-income ratio, employment status, credit history, income, and loan purpose, to categorise applicants into risk groups and forecast default possibilities.

6. Risk Assessment Instruments:

   - Makes use of risk assessment instruments, such as probability of default and credit risk scorecards

   - Uses scenario analysis, sensitivity analysis, and stress testing to assess how market shocks and unfavourable economic conditions affect credit portfolios.

7. Automated Procedures for Underwriting:

   - Automates loan origination, credit approval, and risk assessment procedures by utilising financial analytics tools and decision support systems for underwriting.

   - Makes use of data-driven insights and predictive analytics to streamline operations, cut down on processing times, and increase consistency in decision-making.

Results:

1. Increased Credit Decision Accuracy:

   XYZ Bank has an increase in credit decision accuracy and dependability, which lowers default rates, credit losses, and improves portfolio quality.

2. Enhanced Risk Management:

   The bank can efficiently quantify and manage credit risk, assuring regulatory compliance and preserving financial stability, thanks to predictive credit scoring algorithms and risk assessment tools.

3. Enhanced Operational Efficiency:

   By automating underwriting procedures and integrating financial analytics tools, manual labour is reduced, workflows are streamlined, and organisational productivity is raised.

4. Regulatory Compliance:

   By putting in place strong credit risk management procedures, reporting tools, and governance structures backed by financial analytics, XYZ Bank exhibits compliance with regulatory regulations.

This case study concludes by demonstrating how XYZ Bank used financial analytics to improve credit decision-making, increase credit scoring and risk assessment procedures, and successfully reduce credit risk. The bank improved the accuracy, efficiency, and regulatory compliance of its credit risk management operations by using data-driven insights and sophisticated analytics approaches. This helped the bank position itself for long-term success and growth in the fiercely competitive banking sector.

Case Study: Financial Analytics for Fraud Detection and Prevention

ABC Bank is a major financial organisation that offers a variety of banking services, such as investment services, corporate banking, and retail banking.

By using financial analytics to proactively identify and reduce fraudulent actions, the bank hopes to improve its fraud detection and prevention skills.

Problems:

1. An Increase in Fraud Incidents:

    ABC Bank is seeing an increase in fraudulent transactions, which can result in financial losses and harm to its reputation. These transactions include identity theft, account takeover, credit card fraud, and fraudulent loan applications.

2. Reactive Approach:

    To detect fraud, the bank uses rule-based technology and human processes, which causes delays in spotting fraudulent activity and reacting to new threats.

3. Data Silos:

    The bank's capacity to efficiently analyse and correlate data for fraud detection is hampered by the fact that transactional and customer data are kept in different systems.

4. Regulatory Compliance: ABC Bank is required to adhere to rules, including Know Your Customer (KYC) and Anti-Money Laundering (AML) legislation. These regulations demand the implementation of efficient fraud detection and prevention procedures.

Solution:

ABC Bank uses financial analytics to develop a framework for fraud detection and prevention:

1. Integration and Analysis of Data:

    Integrates data from many sources, such as transaction data, customer information, external data feeds, and past fraud incidences.

Using financial analytics tools and procedures, cleans, validates, and preprocesses the data to guarantee correctness and consistency.

2.   Anomaly Detection:

This method looks for odd patterns or departures from typical behaviour that can point to fraudulent conduct. It does this by applying tools including statistical analysis, machine learning algorithms, and behavioural analytics. It examines network traffic, transactional data, and user behaviour to find anomalies that could be signs of fraud, like huge transactions, odd spending patterns, and shady account access.

3.   Pattern Recognition:

Identifies common fraud patterns and trends across many types of fraudulent activity by applying pattern recognition techniques, such as clustering analysis, association rule mining, and social network analysis. To improve fraud detection skills, analyses past fraud episodes to find reoccurring patterns, fraudster profiles and methods of operation.

4.   Real-Time Monitoring:

This technique uses alerting and monitoring technologies to identify fraudulent activity as it happens and to take prompt action.

Results:

1.   Increased Fraud Detection Accuracy:

ABC Bank reduces financial losses and reputational risks by detecting fraudulent activity with increased accuracy and effectiveness. This results in the early detection and prevention of fraudulent transactions.

2. Improved Operational Efficiency:

   By automating fraud detection procedures and integrating financial analytics technologies, manual labour is reduced, workflows are streamlined, and productivity is increased throughout the company.

3. Proactive Fraud Prevention:

   The bank can proactively detect new fraud patterns and foresee potential threats thanks to real- time monitoring and predictive analytics. This allows for prompt intervention and the prevention of fraudulent activity.

4. Regulatory Compliance:

   ABC Bank uses strong reporting tools, governance structures backed by financial analytics, and fraud detection and prevention techniques to show that it complies with regulatory standards.

To sum up, this case study demonstrates how ABC Bank used financial analytics to improve operational effectiveness, bolster fraud detection and prevention skills, and reduce the financial and reputational risks related to fraudulent activity. In an ever-changing and demanding banking landscape, the bank established itself as a reliable and safe financial partner by adopting data-driven insights and cutting-edge analytics approaches. This allowed the bank to battle fraud with increased precision, agility, and effectiveness.

Case Study: Financial Analytics-Based Customer Segmentation and Targeting

XYZ Bank is a well-known financial company that provides a variety of banking services and products, such as wealth management, investment advisory services, and retail banking. By using financial analytics to gain a deeper understanding of client behaviours, preferences, and needs, the bank hopes to improve its customer segmentation and targeting tactics.

Problems:

1. Lack of Customer Insights:

    XYZ Bank has trouble getting a thorough understanding of the needs, preferences, and behaviours of its customers, which makes their customer segmentation and targeting tactics less than ideal.

2. Ineffective Marketing Campaigns:

    The bank's marketing initiatives are impersonal and irrelevant, which lowers consumer engagement, response rates and saves money.

3. Data Silos:

    The bank's capacity to efficiently analyse and integrate data for client segmentation and targeting is hampered by the fact that customer data is kept in several systems and databases.

4. Competitive Pressure:

    Fintech companies and digital banks are becoming more and more of a threat to XYZ Bank's market share, therefore the bank needs to find new, data-driven strategies for attracting and retaining customers.

Solution:

By utilising financial information, XYZ Bank creates a framework for client segmentation and targeting.

1. Data Integration and Analysis:

    This process combines consumer information from several sources, such as transactional data, demographic data, online activity and social media exchanges. makes use of financial analytics tools and procedures to clean, validate, and preprocess the data in order to guarantee correctness and consistency.

2. Customer Segmentation:

    This method divides customers into groups based on behaviours, demographics, and clustering analysis. Targeted customer groups are developed by identifying segmentation criteria through analysis of customer transactional data, spending patterns, product usage, and life stage events.

3. Predictive Analytics:

    Forecasts consumer behaviour and projects future actions, including product purchases, account closures, or churn, by using predictive modelling techniques, such as lifetime value prediction, churn modelling and propensity modelling.

4. Creates marketing messages, recommendations, and offers that are specifically catered to the requirements and tastes of each consumer segment.

5. Tailored Marketing Campaigns:

    Using insights from consumer segmentation and projections from predictive analytics, tailored marketing campaigns are developed. Makes use of multichannel marketing techniques to connect and interact with consumers at several touchpoints, such as email marketing, social media advertising, direct mail, and customised web experiences.

Outcomes:

1. Better Customer Understanding:

    Through customer segmentation and targeting, XYZ Bank obtains thorough insights into customer behaviours, preferences, and needs, enabling more relevant and personalised interactions.

2. Enhanced Marketing Effectiveness:

    Response rates, consumer engagement, and return on investment (ROI) are all improved by focused marketing efforts that are powered by predictive analytics and customer segmentation.

3. Improved Customer Experience:

    Better customer happiness, loyalty, and retention are the outcome of customized offers and recommendations made to each consumer segment.

4. Competitive Advantage:

    By using financial analytics to produce tailored and data-driven customer experiences, set itself apart from the competition, and fortify customer connections, XYZ Bank gains a competitive advantage in the market.

To sum up, this case study demonstrates how XYZ Bank used financial analytics to boost marketing efficacy, target and segment customers more effectively, and provide individualised customer experiences in the cutthroat banking sector. The bank improved customer knowledge, engagement, and loyalty by adopting data-driven insights and sophisticated analytics tools, setting itself up for long-term success and expansion in a changing and dynamic market environment.

Case Study: Financial Analytics for Regulatory Compliance and Reporting

ABC Financial Services is a global financial company that provides both individual and institutional customers with a comprehensive array of banking and investing solutions. By utilising financial analytics to guarantee compliance with regulations and improve transparency, the organisation hopes to fortify its reporting and regulatory compliance procedures.

Problems:

1. Changing Regulatory Environment:

    Basel III, the Dodd-Frank Act, Know Your Customer (KYC) standards, and other laws are just a few examples of the highly regulated business in which ABC Financial Services operates.

2. Manual Compliance Processes:

    Due to the company's heavy reliance on manual labour, spreadsheet-based analysis, and disjointed systems, regulatory reporting is delayed, erroneous, and inefficient.

3. Data Complexity:

    Compiling and analysing vast amounts of data from various sources, such as transactional data, customer information, market data, and financial statements, is necessary for regulatory reporting. This presents difficulties for data integration and analysis.

4. Compliance Risk:

    ABC Financial Services faces financial and legal risks, such as fines, penalties, harm to its brand, and erosion of client trust, when it fails to comply with regulatory regulations.

Solution:

ABC Financial Services uses financial analytics to build a framework for regulatory compliance and reporting.

1. Data Integration and Analysis:

    Combines data from external sources, such as industry benchmarks and regulatory databases, with data from internal systems, such as accounting, transaction processing, and customer relationship management (CRM) systems. Preprocesses, cleans, and verifies the data to guarantee correctness, consistency, and completeness by utilising financial analytics.

2. Regulatory Compliance Monitoring:

    To keep track of changes to regulations, evaluate compliance risks, and spot non-compliance areas, automated compliance monitoring and alerting systems are put in place. Makes use of regulatory mapping tools, compliance calendars, and regulatory intelligence systems to stay current on changes to regulations and guarantee timely compliance.

3. Regulatory Reporting Automation: To expedite data collection, validation, and submission, regulatory reporting software and financial analytics technologies are used to automate regulatory reporting operations. To guarantee accuracy and consistency in regulatory filings, XBRL (eXtensible Business Reporting Language) tagging, regulatory reporting frameworks, and standardised reporting templates are used.

4. Risk-Based Compliance methods:

    Puts into practice risk-based compliance methods that give high-risk regions priority and efficiently distribute resources to reduce compliance risks.

Results:

1. Enhanced Regulatory Compliance:

    ABC Financial Services attains higher precision, uniformity, and promptness in regulatory reporting, guaranteeing adherence to regulatory mandates and mitigating the likelihood of non- adherence.

2. Improved Operational Efficiency:

    By automating compliance procedures and integrating financial analytics tools, manual labour is reduced, workflows are streamlined, and productivity is increased throughout the company.

3. Lower Risks of Noncompliance:

    The organisation may successfully identify and reduce compliance risks through proactive monitoring of regulatory changes and risk-based compliance methods, thereby protecting itself from potential legal and financial fines.

4. Enhanced Stakeholder Confidence:

    The public's faith in the company's governance and compliance procedures is bolstered by transparent and timely regulatory reporting, which also increases regulatory credibility.

In summary, this case study shows how ABC Financial Services used financial analytics to improve accountability and transparency in the highly regulated financial sector, as well as to reinforce its regulatory compliance and reporting procedures. The organisation increased the efficacy, confidence, and efficiency of its compliance activities by adopting data-driven insights and sophisticated analytics methodologies, setting itself up for long-term success and sustainability in a changing regulatory landscape.

Chapter 12

Challenges in Financial Analytics

In financial institutions, investment firms, and corporations, financial analytics is essential to decision-making. However, obtaining, evaluating, and interpreting financial data can present a number of difficulties. The efficacy, efficiency, and accuracy of financial analytics may be impacted by these difficulties. These are a few of the main challenges

1. Data Accessibility and Quality:

Data that is partial or Inconsistent: Inaccurate analysis and conclusions might result from financial data that is obsolete, partial, or inconsistent across many sources. Data silos: It can be challenging to access and integrate extensive datasets in many organisations since data is kept in different systems or departments. Unstructured Data: A sizable amount of financial data is unstructured (text from news stories, financial reports, etc.), which makes it difficult to extract, process, and analyse.

2. Financial Data Complexity:

High Volume and Velocity: Managing and analysing the massive amount of financial data that is produced every day in real-time might be difficult due to the generation of market data, transaction records, and news.

Complex Instruments: Derivatives and other financial products and instruments have complex structures that make correct modelling and analysis challenging.

Interdependencies: It is difficult to identify individual causes of market behaviour since financial markets are intertwined and have complicated linkages between a variety of factors (such as interest rates, exchange rates, and economic indices).

3. Concerns about Regulation and Compliance:

Regulations That Change All the Time: Organisations that want to be compliant with financial regulations must regularly update their analytical models and processes. Financial regulations change often.

Data privacy: Adhering to data protection laws, such the CCPA or GDPR, may restrict the usage of personal information in financial analytics, making data management and analysis procedures more difficult.

Reporting Requirements: Regulatory authorities frequently demand thorough financial reporting, which can be expensive and time-consuming to complete, especially when several regulatory standards from different countries must be followed.

4. Technological Difficulties:

Integration of Legacy Systems: A lot of financial institutions continue to use outdated systems that are challenging to link with contemporary analytics platforms, which limits the availability of data and the capacity for analysis.

Scalability: Making sure analytical systems and infrastructure can grow efficiently without performance deterioration as data quantities rise is a major concern.

Security concerns: Because financial data is so sensitive, it's critical to keep analytical systems secure to avert data breaches and cyberattacks.

5. Difficulties with Modelling and Analysis:

Financial models are subject to inherent hazards that can arise from inaccurate assumptions, oversimplifications, or an inability to effectively represent market dynamics. These factors can lead to poor analysis and conclusions.

Overfitting: When using predictive analytics, there's a chance that models will be overfit to previous data, which could lead to subpar performance.

Interpretability: Complex and hard to understand advanced analytical methods, like machine learning algorithms, can make it difficult to communicate the findings to stakeholders or regulators.

6. Human Factors

Skill Gaps: The need for financial professionals with tech, data science, and analytics knowledge is rising, but there may not always be enough talent to fill the positions. Human biases have the potential to affect how analytical data are interpreted, which can result in less-than-ideal decisions being made.

Change management is necessary to guarantee that new analytical tools and procedures are adopted and aligned with corporate objectives. Employee opposition to these changes may arise.

7. Resource and Cost Restraints:

High Implementation Costs: Setting up sophisticated financial analytics systems and tools can be expensive, especially for smaller businesses with tighter budgets.

Resource Allocation: It can be difficult to strike a balance between the day-to-day operations and the creation of new analytics capabilities when it comes to the allocation of resources (such as time, money, and personnel).

8. Real-Time Analytics:

Latency Issues: Missed opportunities or less-than-ideal deals can arise from delays in data processing and analytics, particularly in the financial markets where seconds can make a difference.

Data Synchronisation: Accurate analysis depends on real-time synchronisation of data from several sources, yet this can be challenging to accomplish.

9. Moral Points to Remember:

Algorithmic bias: Machine learning-based automated financial analytics systems are particularly prone to unintentionally introducing biases that provide unfair or discriminating results.

Influence on Making Decisions: Concerns of decision-making accountability arise from the potential reduction of human oversight brought about by the growing reliance on automated analytics technologies.

10. Adjusting to Shifts in the Market Uncertainty and Volatility:

Rapid shifts in the market brought about by technical advancements, geopolitical unrest, or economic events might make current models and analytics obsolete.

Model Adaptability: It's a constant struggle to make sure analytical models can swiftly adjust to shifting market conditions without requiring extensive re-engineering.

Conclusion:

A combination of cutting-edge technology, knowledgeable staff, effective data management procedures, and a tactical approach to financial analytics are needed to meet these problems. Businesses who can effectively handle these difficulties will be in a better position to take financial data and turn it into actionable insights, make wise decisions, and stay one step ahead of the competition in the financial sector.

Future Trends in Financial Analytics

The financial analytics domain is undergoing swift transformation, propelled by technological breakthroughs, shifting market conditions, and mounting regulatory obligations. The following are some significant upcoming trends that are anticipated to influence the financial analytics industry:

1. Machine learning and artificial intelligence:

AI-Driven Predictive Analytics: The use of machine learning algorithms to forecast market trends, evaluate credit risk, and automate trading methods will grow in the coming years. These algorithms are capable of quickly analysing enormous volumes of data and finding patterns that people would overlook.

Natural Language Processing (NLP): To assess market sentiment and make better investment decisions, NLP will be utilised to evaluate unstructured data sources such as news articles, social media, and financial reports.

Explainable AI (XAI): As AI models get more sophisticated, there will be an increasing need for explainable AI, which enables analysts and regulators to comprehend how these models make decisions.

2. Distributed ledger technology (DLT) and blockchain:

Improved Data Security and Transparency: Blockchain technology will offer more transparent and safe means to handle financial data and record transactions, lowering the possibility of fraud and enhancing auditability.

Smart Contracts: On blockchain platforms, automated, self-executing contracts will simplify procedures like reporting, compliance, and settlement, improving the efficiency of financial operations.

Decentralised Finance (DeFi): Based on blockchain technology, DeFi platforms are anticipated to expand, presenting new chances and difficulties for financial analytics, especially in the fields of risk management and legal compliance.

3. Advanced Analytics and Big Data:

Real-Time Analytics: In fields like risk management, fraud detection, and high-frequency trading, the capacity to handle and analyse massive amounts of data in real-time will be crucial. Data Lakes and Cloud Computing: By utilising data lakes and cloud-based solutions, businesses will be able to store and process large amounts of data more effectively, leading to more advanced analytics and decision-making.

Other Sources of Data: Analysts will employ alternate data sources (such as satellite imagery, geolocation data, and social media activity) in addition to traditional financial data more often in order to improve predictive models and obtain deeper insights.

4. Speed and Efficiency of Quantum Computing:

Particularly in areas like portfolio optimisation, quantum computing has the potential to completely transform financial analytics by tackling complicated problems far more quickly than traditional computers.

Quantum Algorithms for Finance: As quantum computing advances, it's possible that specialised quantum algorithms with previously unheard-of accuracy and speed will be developed to address certain financial issues.

5. Tailored Financial Services:

Robo-Advisors: AI-powered robo-advisors will keep developing, providing highly individualised portfolio management and investment advising services based on each client's unique financial objectives, risk tolerance, and market circumstances. Customer-Centric Analytics: Financial institutions will employ cutting-edge analytics to provide more individualised services and products, like retirement plans, insurance policies, and loan offers that are specific to each customer's needs.

6. RegTech (Regulatory Technology) Automated Compliance:

Using AI and machine learning to monitor transactions, identify anomalies, and provide reports, RegTech solutions will be increasingly used by financial institutions to automate compliance with regulatory standards.

Real-Time Reporting: Companies may be compelled by regulatory agencies to disclose financial transactions and risk exposures in real-time, which forces them to invest in increasingly advanced data management and analytics systems.

Data Security and Privacy: In order to abide by strict laws like the CCPA and GDPR, analytics platforms will need to incorporate sophisticated encryption and data anonymisation methods. This is because worries about data privacy are becoming more and more pressing.

7. Environmental, Social, and Governance (ESG) Analytics and Sustainability Integration of ESG Metrics:

As demand for sustainable investing grows, financial analytics will progressively integrate ESG elements into risk assessment, performance evaluation, and investment decision-making. Modelling Climate Risk: To evaluate and simulate the financial effects of climate change on assets, portfolios, and company operations, analytics tools will be created. Impact investing: In order to help investors match their investments with their values, analytics will be used more frequently to assess the social and environmental effects of investments.

8. Improved visuals and user experience (UX) Interactive Dashboards:

In order to facilitate data exploration, insight generation, and decision-making, financial analytics platforms will provide more user-friendly and interactive dashboards.

Virtual reality (VR) and augmented reality (AR): These technologies can be combined to produce immersive data visualisation experiences that aid in the understanding of complicated financial data and situations by analysts and decision-makers. Voice-Activated Analytics: With advancements in voice recognition technology, voice- activated financial analytics systems that enable users to engage with data and do analysis through natural language commands are likely to become more common.

9. Ethical and Responsible AI Bias Mitigation:

To guarantee just and moral results, there will be an increased emphasis on detecting and reducing biases in models as AI and machine learning proliferate in financial analytics. AI Governance: To guarantee accountability and transparency, organisations must set up strong governance frameworks for AI, which should include rules for model development, validation, and monitoring.

Sustainability of AI Models: As the environmental effects of large-scale AI models become more widely recognised, there may be a movement in financial analytics towards more sustainable and energy-efficient AI solutions.

10. Financial Openness and Collaborative Analytics

Open Banking APIs:

As open banking frameworks are adopted further, more collaborative analytics will be possible, allowing financial institutions, fintechs, and outside suppliers to exchange data and jointly develop cutting-edge financial goods and services.

Collaborative Platforms: Teams from many organisations and locations will be able to collaborate in real-time on intricate financial models and analyses thanks to cloud-based collaborative analytics platforms.

Conclusion

The future of financial analytics is poised to be shaped by rapid technological advancements, increasing data availability, and evolving market and regulatory landscapes. Organizations that can leverage these trends to enhance their analytics capabilities will be better positioned to gain a competitive edge, manage risks effectively, and meet the growing demands of their clients and stakeholders.

List of Abbreviations

NPV	Net present value
ARR	Average Rate of Return
TEFR	Techno- economic feasibility report
IPO	Initial Public Offering
GDPR	General Data Protection Regulation
FINRA	Financial Industry Regulatory Authority
IOT	Internet of Things
CPS	Cyber-Physical Systems
AR	Augmented Reality
VR	Virtual Reality
ROI	Return on Investment
DCF	Discounted Cash flow
CCPA	California Consumer Privacy Act
ARIMA	Autoregressive Integrated Moving Average
GARCH	Generalized Autoregressive Conditional Heteroskedasticity
MAD	Mean Absolute Deviation
IQR	The interquartile range
VaR	Value at Risk
AI	Artificial Intelligence
ML	Machine learning
SVR	Support Vector Regression
SVM	Support vector machines
PCA	Principal Component Analysis
KPI	Key Performance Indicators
DBMS	Database Management Systems

IMS	Information Management System
CRM	Customer relationship management
ERP	Enterprise Resource Planning
ER	Entity Relationship
SQL	Structured Query Language
DCL	Data Control Language
DML	Data Manipulation Language
DDL	Data Definition Language
Amazon RDS	Amazon Relational Database Service
CRAN	Comprehensive R Archive Network
TTR	Technical Trading Rules
ARIMA	Autoregressive Integrated Moving Average
VaR	Value at Risk
AML	Anti-Money Laundering
FP&A	Financial Planning and Analysis
SMA	Simple Moving Average
CVaR	Conditional Value at Risk
LCR	Liquidity Coverage Ratio
KYC	Know Your Customer
XBRL	Extensible Business Reporting Language
DLT	Distributed Ledger Technology
XAI	Explainable AI
DeFi	Decentralized Finance
ESG	Environmental, Social, and Governance
APIs	Application Programming Interface